Taking Flight

TAKING FLIGHT

THE GUIDE TO COLLEGE FOR DIVERSE LEARNERS AND NON-TRADITIONAL STUDENTS

PERRY LAROQUE, PHD

NEW YORK

LONDON • NASHVILLE • MELBOURNE • VANCOUVER

TAKING FLIGHT

THE GUIDE TO COLLEGE FOR DIVERSE LEARNERS AND NON-TRADITIONAL STUDENTS

Published in New York, New York, by Morgan James Publishing. Morgan James is a trademark of Morgan James, LLC. www.MorganJamesPublishing.com

Some of the stories have been modified to fit the format of the book, but they maintain the integrity of the story as originally told

Morgan James BOGO™

A **FREE** ebook edition is available for you or a friend with the purchase of this print book.

CLEARLY SIGN YOUR NAME ABOVE

Instructions to claim your free ebook edition:
1. Visit MorganJamesBOGO.com
2. Sign your name CLEARLY in the space above
3. Complete the form and submit a photo of this entire page
4. You or your friend can download the ebook to your preferred device

ISBN 9781642796063 paperback
ISBN 9781642796070 eBook
Library of Congress Control Number:
2019941626

Cover Design by:
DesignerName
www.website.com

Interior Design by:
DesignerName
www.website.com

Morgan James is a proud partner of Habitat for Humanity Peninsula and Greater Williamsburg. Partners in building since 2006.

Get involved today! Visit
MorganJamesPublishing.com/giving-back

For Emily, of course.

CONTENTS

FOREWORD

The first bonus gift parents are given when we are told that our children have been diagnosed with Autistic Spectrum Disorder is, "Oh, and by the way, there is no cure. Your daughter or son has Autism and he or she will always have it." Yet, no matter how clearly that fact is repeatedly drilled into us by medical professionals, we don't buy it. In fact, our lives as parents immediately turn into a mission to defy that reality – to overcome the diagnosis. And when we finally do come to grips with the reality that our children won't overcome their diagnoses; we don't stop there. We attempt to enable our children with the skills to conceal their differences. To hide in plain sight. We work very hard to have their differences become undetectable to the world at large. We seek to have our children "mainstreamed", we hope that they will be able to "blend", have neurotypical friends, and fly under the radar. We start to measure their success by how well they fit in. How little they *appear* to be different. I remember secretly envying parents whose child "fit in" better than mine, and feeling sympathy (and perhaps a degree of schadenfreude) for parents whose child stood out more than my own.

It is only with the gift of time and perspective that I can plainly see how misguided I was, and so many of us parents were. Playing the game of making our children fit into a world that they were not born to fit into was a game where we could only lose.

I ask myself now why was I so obsessed with my child being, or at least appearing to be, normal? *Me* of all people. As a teenager, I fully embraced my own differences. I was not autistic, but grew up in disco-obsessed 1970's Brooklyn where I was a folk-singing hippie. John Travolta was our Brooklyn-bred God, yet I walked out twenty minutes into Saturday Night Fever (a movie I eventually grew to love), and instead traipsed around my neighborhood in torn jeans, leather hats, long unruly hair, guitar slung over my shoulder and cut many classes to learn to play Bob Dylan songs. (A past-time I continue to enjoy.) In fact, a natural extension of my identity as an outlier was to become a playwright after college, which led to a career writing and creating television shows. Embracing my own *other-ness* became my path to success.

Yet for my own son – why could I not embrace his inner other-ness? Why did I need him to be normal? In retrospect, I can say for certain that my desire for my son to fit in had nothing to do with him and everything to do with me. If I could change one thing about the way I raised my son from the time I learned of his diagnosis, I would change my own need for him to fit in with the world.

Not to blame myself. It came understandably from a core parental instinct to protect our children from the big, bad world. It came from the fear that he would be isolated, singled out, alone, and lonely. Ironically, none of what I did changed an iota of the outcome. Today, my son in all his beauty certainly does not fit in. It is only now, after twenty-two years that I've come to realize that I've been chasing the wrong dream all along. I've been trying to make my son understand the world, when in fact, it's the other way around. The world needs to understand him. Looking back now at all those years, all of that worry and pressure put on him to try to sound, think and act like other kids, I wish I could have said to myself, to my son and to anyone who asked – "Screw normal".

But I couldn't. I couldn't do that because consciously or unconsciously I was in a race. By the time he graduated high school, he needed to be normal.

In fairness to me, and my fellow parents, this race was not born only out of our own psychological desire of wanting our children to grow into their own by the time they graduated high school. It was embedded in the system, the culture and the law. The law requires the government to provide an education for every child, no matter their ability. Until the student receives a high school diploma, public schools must help support us with resources, accommodations, special schools, shadows, and funding for therapeutic services and aides. But once my son graduated high school and became an "adult", the government was more or less done helping out. It was time for him to leave the nest and fly.

Well, needless to say, that didn't happen.

As my son graduated from high school, his future seemed less clear than many of his neurodiverse peers, some of whom were destined to thrive in college, others who would never see a college classroom and, instead, begin to focus on a vocational path. Our son was a tweener. He wasn't a savant who scored a perfect score on his SATs and could finish the Sunday New York Times crossword puzzle in mere minutes. But at the same time, he wasn't necessarily headed on a vocational tract. He was smart and intellectually curious and had aspirations for college. And we had aspirations for him to go to college.

Yet, as much as our son bought into the myth that he was eighteen and ready to be autonomous, the reality is he was someone who was going to need a tremendous amount of support to succeed in college or get to the next stage in life.

We found that support for a young man like our son was very hard to find.

Though it was very clearly stated in the diagnosis that Autism and related disorders are lifelong diagnoses, our society as a whole seemed to be engaged in a universal denial system. There were relatively few universities and colleges that had programs that would embrace, support or even consider admitting students like our son. And those that did were well hidden and hard to find. Many schools had offices for students with disabilities, but in digging into them, sometimes they seemed to be sorely lacking practical supports that we know our son and students like him need.

So, while other friends with neurotypical kids were going on school tours throughout the country deciding whether they wanted a big sports school, a small liberal arts school; whether they wanted the Northeast, or West Coast; whether they wanted to go pre-med or just party for four years – we went on a much different kind of search. A search of "Is there somewhere? Is there *anywhere* in this country that has a place that will embrace our son?"

Even the very adept educational expert we hired to help place him didn't have a solution that felt right. The programs all felt like they were either too academically challenging for our son, or not academically ambitious enough – giving lip service to having their students have college opportunities, when they were really being put on a vocational track. Where was a program that valued the intellectual potential for someone like our son, but was up for the task of continuing to help him develop the executive functioning and life skills he dearly needed to succeed in this next stage of life?

We searched far and wide. As Woody Guthrie put it, we did some hard travelin'. Eventually we went from our home in Southern California to Northern Vermont, about as far as you could go within the continental United States. And when we got there, we found Perry LaRoque and Mansfield Hall.

What became clear moments into talking to Perry was his deep well of compassion and belief in diverse learners. Perry wasn't talking down to our son, or to us about him. That was simply not in Perry's DNA as a person, an administrator, or an educator. It was both cathartic and annoying that after talking to my son for only a few minutes, Perry seemed to understand him better than I did after a lifetime of trying to figure out what makes him tick. I don't know what Perry's secret is, but here's my guess – respect. I think he comes to every student with a respect for them at a deep and authentic level.

In short order, Perry and Mansfield Hall became a two-year home to my son. And through their guidance, it led to a new way of how we thought about our son, and I think how he thought about himself.

Through Perry and his team, they helped our son, as they helped so many students, find their voice, allow themselves to be their true selves, and then figure out strategies of how to best present themselves to the world in all their idiosyncratic glory.

Our son is now enrolled as a matriculated student in college, slowly but steadily working toward his BA. They've helped him know how to do it, where to do it, and what is the right pace for him. They threw out the book of assumptions. Perhaps, this semester nine credits are plenty. Perhaps, next summer, enrolling in a couple of classes could be even more productive than lying around on your parents' couch.

There was a time when our son was a teenager that I doubted he would ever take a single college level class. It has taken him awhile, but he now is two-thirds of the way toward his BA.

One of the most common lines I've heard about parenting is, when you come home from the hospital with your child no one gives you a user manual. You have to figure it out on your own. Well, it's similar when you have a neurodiverse child high school grad, who is trying to figure out their post-high-school path. Four years ago, there was no user manual. We had to figure it all out on our own. Well, now there is a user manual. A damn good one.

In *Taking Flight: An Insider's Guide to College for Diverse Learners*, Perry LaRoque has coalesced his gifts as an educator, administrator, and behavior specialist to create a cohesive, well written, and essential guide for any diverse learner (and their parents/support teams) who seeks higher education. He's taken the knowledge and help we were grateful to find those years ago, and made it accessible to everyone. The pages are filled with sage wisdom and guidance on virtually every aspect of the experience, from choosing the right program to finding and utilizing support and accommodations, to achieving success – both academically and socially. He tells these stories with humor, empathy and honesty and uses a plethora of definitive examples from the mouths and minds of diverse learners who have lived through and experienced where the reader is about to go.

Taking Flight is good. It is good because of the wisdom, advice, facts, and tricks that it shares with the reader. It is good because it brings that information to you with humor and empathy. But mostly, it is good because it is told with a voice that will embolden and encourage you to embrace your true self, follow your dreams, and understand that sometimes it's not you that has to fit in with the rest of the world, but the rest of the world that needs to fit in with you.

Jason Katims, Creator and Executive Producer of the NBC series *Parenthood*

INTRODUCTION:

Learning, Living, Giving, and Engaging

If you ask a roomful of college graduates the most important thing they learned in college, generally, not one person in the room talks about what they learned in the classroom. You get a lot of *responsibility, passion, love, working with others, beer pong, organizational skills, what I didn't want to do, happiness,* but you don't get biomechanical microbiological primate philosophical mathematical science. This is the elephant in the classroom.

Everyone says you should go to college to get a diploma and then have a meaningful career. Rarely is that what they value about their own time at university. College is much more than just studying, exams, textbooks and long lectures. In fact, if that's all it was, no one would go. The information you learn at college exists online, everywhere, for much less hassle. So, why is the promise of college so reliably fostered by every generation? College is a holistic adventure and thus, to be truly successful in college, you must foster all dimensions of the college experience.

If you think of a truly successful college experience, there are four core dimensions that emerge, specifically: *learning, engaging, living, and giving back.* First, the boring stuff. Everyone expects to "hit the books" in college. You take classes, you study, you do assignments and projects, and you take exams. You are learning. This is the area that most people claim is the most important. It's certainly the most expensive aspect. However, if you stay at home and take all of your classes online, you will have missed the most essential parts of the college experience.

Which brings us to the second core dimension. Generally, people have fun in college by *engaging* in the community. This may be getting involved in sports, clubs, political movements or hobbies. This is where you learn to socialize and interact with other like-minded, motivated people. And because there are so many students, you're incredibly lucky to be forced to deal with many unlike-minded folks, too. College students begin dating and having girlfriends and boyfriends and then they break up and do it again. That's how they learn to eventually be good husbands and wives. So, I guess all this engaging can lead to engagements. But, it's more important that you are making friends and being as social as you find comfortable.

Third, college is where students learn to live independently. Basically, instead of pretending to play house, you actually get to play house. You actually get to do this living thing. This is not only the time you get to choose your favorite tapestry or poster to proudly display in your room, but it's also your first opportunity to actually begin doing the tasks your parents nagged you about and warned would be all yours in the not-too-distant future. Students slowly learn how to cook, clean, live with other people, manage their money, and pay their bills. Simply put, this is the time most people grow up. By convention this is now called "adulting."

Finally, students develop a world perspective and vocational skills through giving back. Giving back can be volunteering, internships, work study, community involvement and part time jobs. Indeed, a successful college student incorporates all four of these dimensions and without attention to each, you leave experiences on the table necessary for a truly successful college experience.

So, this isn't a book about getting good grades, this is a book about having a successful college experience. This is about navigating through an unfamiliar landscape and learning how to make it work for you. This is about learning to balance those four dimensions and creating a diverse experience that travels with you for life. Don't think that because you are highly intelligent and aced every exam in high school that you will skip your way through a college degree, and likewise, even if you found high school to be challenging you may still be well on your way to a very successful college experience — if you can master the elements discussed in this book. College is not high school 2.0; it is radically different in scope, opportunity, and consequence. You must strive for success in all aspects of the college experience to truly find its value. But, it's important to remember that you can't do it on your own.

All of you will be bringing a few companions on this ride, whether it's your parents, siblings, former teachers, or friends. No, they won't be coming to class with you, but they are the ones who will be your closest advisers, loudest cheerleaders, and provide you with the most frank and sometimes painful feedback. Hopefully, they are also reading this book, so that they will know how to help, when to advocate, and how your path will be unique.

Conceptually, this book should serve as your instruction manual to the most complex vehicle you have ever encountered, but it remains yours to drive. College is more, and must be more, than just what you learn in class; the college experience is learning, it's living, it's engaging, and it's giving back.

CHAPTER 1:

The System is Definitely Not Made for You

"The doors are open, the opportunities are yours for the taking, the time is right, but you must know one extremely important thing—no one is going to do it for you."

---

*D*rew Maxwell started off elementary school eager and excited *like every other kid living in the suburbs of Milwaukee. He anticipated that school would be the wonderful place that he saw on television. It would be where his dreams were realized and his successes endless. But that ended in 2nd grade when his dreams were crushed by the evil beast, "Spelling."*

"I'd spend more time contemplating why in the world 'of' was pronounced like 'uv' and not like 'off.' It didn't make any sense. Even today, when I'm writing or reading and I come to one of those

ridiculous 'there, their, or they're' traps, I can't help but think, why would they do this to us!?"

Drew's comprehensive inability to spell landed him an invite to participate in "special" education down the hall. He remembers walking into "that room" for the first time and seeing everyone who was bad at school, all in the same place.

"It was like they were saying, because you are slow in spelling, we are going to treat you like an idiot." He was surrounded by students with a wide variety of disabilities, most students requiring way more help than he did.

"There were people with physical disabilities in that classroom. I mean smart kids with physical disabilities. I was like, I can't spell, how is that similar to not walking?"

But "that room" was for the school's losers in Drew's mind, the folks that didn't make the grade. Drew's self-esteem plummeted — he wondered if poor spellers really were stupid, and he became totally disengaged in school. But alongside, he also thought, "I'm sitting in the classroom looking at the teacher and thinking, 'I'm way smarter than you, I just can't spell.'"

The frustration and disappointment in this formal discrediting were clear to Drew from a young age. Every day he was shamefully dismissed from the classroom with his "regular" peers while they did activities deemed too difficult for him. His motivation and dreams began slipping away. He felt like he had so much to contribute, but was stuck in an industrial model of schooling that was fast-tracking him toward a life of menial labor. Drew felt chained to what others called his "disability."

Compounded with a difficult move to a new school and the entry into the pubescent Hell known as middle school, things got even worse in his teens. Drew formed a negative identity in opposition to the student he had hoped he would be.

"I felt pretty much hopeless, until the school psychologist wanted to talk with me. I started to get to know him better and I'd play cards in

his office and he'd take me out to lunch. One day as I was sitting in his office, he turned and looked at me and said, 'You know Drew, you are really smart.' I immediately got defensive, as this was something I had become accustomed to only believing on my own. I said, no I'm not and he said he'd prove it to me and give me an IQ test. I was like nooooo, I'm not taking a test! But he convinced me and said he would bet I was smarter than every teacher in the building. I thought he was hilarious."

Sure enough, Drew's IQ test confirmed what he had known deep down all along, he was a genius. The psychologist said to Drew, 'you are the only person in this building that has ever explained to me what a black hole is, that makes you pretty damn smart.' The IQ test also confirmed that Drew had dyslexia, a significant deficit in his ability for reading comprehension and phonetic awareness, or basically why "of" sounds like "uv". The school psychologist explained to Drew that this didn't make him dumb, it made him learn differently. As he remembers the psychologist explaining, "this isn't your problem. You are just stuck in a society which is focused on educating the masses. Your brain wants to go fast in a world of molasses. It's the world that's stopping you." It was the first time that it all made sense to him and he determined to "learn to navigate through this bullshit."

Drew Maxwell *(43), Graphic Designer, Comic Book Author, Movie Producer, Artist*

Drew's story of not fitting into the norm is one of many because public education in America is a relatively new notion; we're still trying to work out the best way to do it. Millions of students struggle through school every day as a result of their disabilities, diverse learning needs, or outstanding situations in life. For many, it seems that this struggle in school is a new phenomenon. However, prior to the early 1900's, children weren't even required to attend school.

In the 19th century, children who were privileged, male, white and rich enough to attend school received their education from mostly private parochial schools. Most of these students finished their education by 8th grade. Then, they sought careers, marriages and children.

You can imagine the parental lecture across the country in the 1800's, "It's time to grow up: get a job, find a partner, have children, move out of our house. Enough playing around. I didn't send you to middle school, so you could play with your tinker toys for the rest of your life. Put that tobacco pipe down and listen to me, you are FIFTEEN now, for goodness sake. It's time to make something out of your life!"

In 1918, all states finally required every child to attend school, and the public elementary education system saw a dramatic rise in enrollment. High school and college were reserved for the brightest or richest students. Those students would become our doctors, lawyers and politicians. In fact, until the 1900's, the only majors for college study were liberal arts, law, medicine, and theology.

As high school participation slowly became the norm for adolescents in the late 1900's, college began to play the role of differentiating the future "collars." Blue collar jobs were working class, and white-collar jobs were part of the intellectual class. In 1965, less than 10% of Americans had a college degree, by 2010 that number had more than tripled[1]. As more and more students began to pursue postsecondary education, college, instead of high school, quickly became the standard for the finish line of a traditional education.

As the demand for college has increased, the supply of colleges nationwide has likewise dramatically multiplied. In 1860, there were less than 200 colleges in the United States. Today there are over 5000 colleges with an annual enrollment of over 17 million.

Historically, students picked colleges based on the careers they were interested in. If you wanted to be a lawyer, you'd go to Harvard or Yale; a doctor, maybe Northwestern; a radical tree hugging protester, University of Wisconsin[2]. However, as colleges began competing for students, the model

---

1   http://www.familyfacts.org/charts/560/the-percentage-of-college-graduates-has-soared-since-1965

2   Please read the author's bio before taking offense.

changed to providing an ever-increasing number of specializations. This consumer-driven approach began to cater to student interests and capitalize on offering an education in the most contemporary and attractive fields, such as computer programming or video game design. In Jeffrey Selingo's enlightening evaluation of higher education *College (Un)bound*, he posits that this change in paradigm has created a profit-driven market, where rather than focusing on outcomes, colleges are focused on admissions.

While this was happening, the inclusive movement in public schools became the standard, so that students with disabilities were encouraged to participate in the mainstream. Gone are the days of special education being offered entirely in separate, self-contained classrooms in most public schools. Gone are the days of a learning disability, autism or other developmental disabilities automatically preventing a student from pursuing their self-determined career goals. And gone are the days of a disability, as Temple Grandin would say, being a "less-than" label.

Obviously, the field of education has a long way to go, but these ideals are and should be driving the education of not only diverse learners, but all willing learners. As more diverse learners begin to take their well-deserved and rightful path toward college, the college landscape is being forced to change, by you and the millions of diverse learners who exercise your civil right for education.

With the growing competition for students, colleges have expanded their definition of a "typical" college student. They are being forced to balance the services that cater to these students with the pressure to be sustainable or even profitable. In many colleges nationwide, this has resulted in a reduction in rejections from the college Admissions Office and paradoxically, a reduction or at least not an equivalent growth in the necessity of academic and disability services needed to support this new diverse group of students. Consequently, colleges are finding themselves in a conundrum where they are incapable of serving a cross-section of the students they have worked so hard to recruit.

So, are all colleges ready for you? The short answer is "no, but..."; don't let this discourage you. Many professors and administrators still view college as a place where the most talented students attend to be groomed for the most prestigious careers. Colleges are still judged and evaluated by criteria that ranks their incoming students by standardized assessment scores, GPA, graduation rates and retention. It's in many colleges' best interests to continue to strive to recruit the most capable "on paper" college students. But, given that college has become the norm for high school graduates, the paradigm must and will shift. Quite simply, college needs to become a place where people who want to learn have the greatest opportunity to learn.

Colleges are not a place of teaching, but an institution of learning. Learning is dictated by willingness, interest, and desire, not by intelligence, test scores, or traditional learning characteristics. College should be a place where students have fertile opportunities to learn. While this new college paradigm slowly infiltrates the traditional system, it will require your commitment to not only prove that college is for you, but also require you to work from within, assertively pushing that system to remain nimble and responsive.

The doors are open, the opportunities are yours for the taking, the time is right, but you must know one extremely important thing — no one is going to do it for you. This is your time to rise up and continue to change the system. This is your moment to pave the way for others who learn differently and see the world through unique lenses. This is your opportunity to not only prove the naysayers wrong, but more importantly, prove yourself right. And to smooth the path for the folks following in your footsteps.

College will not be the warm and cozy nest with a basement full of video games and cheesy puffs magically restocked in your cabinet that you may have come to expect. You are about to get nudged out of your proverbial nest, so it's time to spread your wings and take flight. And if you have never seen a bird leave the nest, you are probably thinking of a majestic eagle soaring over amber fields of grain, but what you are actually seeing is a fuzzy, clumsy bird getting smacked by branches, running into trees, and struggling to achieve what appears to come effortlessly, "naturally" to the older birds in the neighborhood.

College is not easy; it is not instinctive. But, don't forget that college is not easy for anyone, it's just that some possess the strengths that the colleges were designed for and can learn to take flight a little quicker. You absolutely have the ability to take flight, but it will take perseverance, passion, hard work, patience, humor, a strong backbone, networks of support and most importantly, the undying belief that you can do it.

Because, you can do it.

Take-Aways:

- Although colleges are changing to meet the growing diverse population of learners, many of the systems were not created in your favor.
- You must learn to overcome the system.

CHAPTER 2:

Identity

"Your journey through college will be as much about learning new things, as it will be coming to know yourself."

---

*B*ack to Drew...

From a young age, Drew was a talented artist. He loved sketching monsters, aliens and action heroes. He found a lot of pride and self-esteem in his art and began to focus more on his talents than dwell on his challenges. Ironically, Drew recalls "I was sitting in art class and drawing these intricate characters and I'd look at what other people were drawing and I'd think 'what the Hell is wrong with you, why can't you draw? They need special education for these guys'.

As he found his passion in art, he still struggled in the rest of his classes. He decided to transfer to a School of the Arts his junior year, in hopes that he would find the inspiration he was missing in his traditional school, but to no avail.

"Teachers kept wanting me to fit into their box and see the world their way. Plus, they were terrible teachers, like illegally terrible teachers. You know it's a bad school when you are skipping out to sneak to the public library to read art history books." Obviously, *conventional schooling was not inspiring Drew.*

Drew begrudgingly graduated high school and decided to enter his art portfolio into an open college recruitment event. He wasn't sure where he wanted to go or if anyone would want him, but he decided to give it a try. By the end of the event, he had 17 full ride offers, including one to the Chicago Art Institute, where they would offer him to skip freshman and sophomore year, and actually start as a junior.

"I was really excited, so I told them I wanted to specialize in digital media. It was the early '90's so digital media was at the cusp of a revolution. They told me that they didn't offer that program, so I called some professors to see if they would sponsor me on this endeavor and I kept hearing the same thing: 'digital media is not art'. Not one of the colleges that was recruiting me offered it as a degree program. I was so disappointed; it was like traditional schooling was destined to fail me. I could see exactly what I wanted out of it, but couldn't quite reach it. "I had an angry vendetta toward traditional education and I was determined to seek my revenge."

Drew decided that he would go it alone and craft his own education. He had experienced so much success and happiness in his life already, despite his experiences in school. He had the support of his friends and former mentors who truly believed in him. This was the moment where Drew relied on his conviction that he would not be handicapped by his disability, and prove to himself that he could succeed in a world not tailored for his uniqueness. He purchased a state-of-the-art computer with a blazing 32mb processor and 8mb of RAM (it was the 90s), along with a pressure sensitive pad for drawing and set out on his own. He studied from whatever resources he could find on digital media, seeking and creating his own accommodations for his disability. As he began to learn how to learn, both his talents and his confidence began to rise. Drew created his own personal school in local coffee shops, parks and his kitchen.

Drew decided to start sharing his talents once he was confident with his skills and began doing freelance work for companies who needed illustrations, graphics or cover art. He even found the confidence to begin taking some art classes at various local colleges.

"Now that I knew how to learn, I was so much more comfortable entering a traditional classroom and advocating for what I needed, without the shame it had brought me before." His business and reputation began to grow. He began publishing graphic novels and comic books, including the acclaimed, "Atomic Fist Punch."

As he experienced financial success and the recognition that comes with it, he also decided to follow through on another of his "wild" ideas. Drew wrote a movie script, something he admits wouldn't have been possible without spellcheck and the watchful eye of his wife. "The Sleeper", the story of CIA spies who enter people's dreams, was immediately picked up, and his script was sent to production. Furthermore, he was asked by the producers to write and create a series of science fiction movies; to do this, he created Lightning Rod Studios, the largest feature film production company in Milwaukee, WI.

Drew began writing and directing movies with titles like Shadowlands, Derelict, and Carnivorous. "The movies, they're like awesome bad science fiction movies with crazy monsters and aliens that are televised in the middle of the night, but are popular around the world. It was like a 10-year old's dream. At one point, I was like 'let's use that gun from Predator', so we called up and rented it from the studio. It was so awesome."

Surprisingly, the kid who couldn't spell and was told public education was not right for him was hired to be a professor at the Milwaukee Institute of Art and Design (MIAD) and recently was named the Executive Director of the MIAD Innovation Center, where he has created programs for film animation and sequential storytelling, a fancy way of saying comic books. He was finally able to begin to right the wrongs from his own schooling experience for other diverse learners. "The way I see it, the whole world loves chocolate cake. If you don't like chocolate, you are in trouble. But there are so many of us out there that just don't like chocolate cake and now I can be the one to say that it doesn't have to matter."

Drew allows his students to see the world through their own lenses and to jump through their own hoops. "I tell them if they want to truly learn, go touch a hot stove. You'll learn not to touch that hot stove really quickly. But the trouble is that the world is full of hot stoves and you have to touch them and learn from being burned each time." He doesn't allow his students to get distracted by disability, but to honor and respect that they learn differently. And that learning differently can lead to great things.

Drew's revenge on public education was never giving up, and being relentless in his belief that he could succeed, against the odds of a system that tried to obstruct his pursuit of a meaningful life. Drew's revenge was to prove that his diverse learning abilities were simply strengths, overshadowed by unfair expectations. Drew's revenge was to prove he could do it.

However, looking back, Drew wouldn't change a thing about himself or his experiences. The challenges and struggles he had in life equipped him to seek his success. He would never trade his learning differences for mainstream intelligence, as he views his differences as an opportunity to see the world in a diverse way and continues to allow him to have an imagination and creativity that most people could never dream uv [sic].

"I tell my students that I'm going to give them a machete and drop them off in the middle of a jungle with no trails. It's their job to learn to use their machete to forge their own path. If they run into dead ends, it's their job to find their bearings and continue navigating through the dense jungle. If I tell them how to get out, they'll only know how to do it my way. Then, when they get out into the world,

they'll be in the middle of another jungle but without a machete. I want to train my students to be badass ninjas who will go out and destroy the world to make it better and more beautiful for everyone. That's what I did, I hope."

Drew Maxwell *(46), Executive Director, Graphic Designer, Comic Book Author, Movie Producer, Artist*

Imagine you just walked into your psychologist's office. Across the room there is a long leather couch that you slowly and awkwardly lie on. As you look up at your shrink, you are terrified when you realize that it's YOU looking back. It makes sense because you should be your best analyst. You should work to understand your motives, desires, drives, and challenges. However, you will also be your toughest client. Basically, you will need to first understand yourself in order to know what will make you successful in college. That's tough, right? But, here's the thing: there are tools that work. There are values that you can adopt and apply that will help you be successful in college and life. These values are Awareness, Regulation, Expression and Dynamic Determination.

Awareness, Regulation, Expression and Dynamic Determination should work in harmony. Without the right balance, your ability to be successful will be greatly hindered. Think of these values as a cycle. Without proper attention to each value, your progress is impeded. Say for instance that you really get how the brakes work on your car, but are iffy on the whole acceleration thing. Essentially, you will hold yourself back from where you want to go. Of course, if you are all about the gas pedal, but fuzzy on the whole braking thing, you'll be looking at a very different, unbalanced problem. So, let's look at the values you'll need to adopt and put them together in a system that works for you.

Awareness

Do you ever have those moments where you're washing your face or brushing your teeth and suddenly you look in the mirror and see yourself looking back and there's a moment of shock? This isn't the pimple popping reflection, it's the "by God, is that me?" reflection. We look in the mirror every day, but every once in a while, we actually see ourselves looking back. As you begin to examine your striking good looks, you may start to wonder if you see yourself the way that others see you. You turn your head from left to right to see both ears. Look up and down to see first your chin and then your forehead. It's hard not to reflect on the "you" that others know, rather than the "you" who looks out from behind your eyes. These are moments of awareness.

Awareness, or self-awareness, is essential for identifying and "owning" your strengths, weaknesses, likes, dislikes, preferences, and desires. More importantly, once you are able to identify those characteristics, understanding how these filters interact and affect your world experience is essential. For example, you may be an excellent writer, but hate writing. You may be fascinated by the Arctic Circle, but hate reading about it. Maybe you love reading, but only science fiction. John Muir famously said, "When we try to pick out anything by itself, we find it hitched to everything else in the Universe." Accordingly, for any weakness or shortcoming a person has, life has a way of developing solutions in areas that offset those challenges. People who lose their vision later in life often report a significant increase in their senses of smell, hearing, and taste. Sometimes these complementary characteristics aren't quite that obvious, and sometimes the "work-around" doesn't substitute perfectly. For those who have troubles writing, their ability to present information verbally may be superior. For those who have difficulty reading, listening to the information may be a strength. It's your job, and secret weapon, to contemplate, examine, and identify these complementary skills and understand how they can be used to your advantage.

So, how is this relevant? I suppose you could find a large tree on a mountain and sit under it while you contemplate your awareness, and seek enlightenment. It worked for the Buddha. However, you may not have that kind of time. Often, we are more aware than we realize. It's purely a matter of taking the time to think about it. Below is a list of some important characteristics with specific questions for being successful in college for you to be aware of. You may be able to answer many of these easily. They will become a list of your strengths and weaknesses. Other questions may not be as easy to answer. They will become your list of characteristics to ponder and reflect on over time.

- **Executive functioning** - How proficient are you at managing your day-to-day responsibilities?
- **Metacognition** - Are you able to think about how you learn?
- **Time Awareness and Self-discipline** - Are you able to dedicate the right amount of time to a series of tasks to stay on schedule?
- **Organization Skills** - Do you have strategies for keeping your life in order?

- **Personal Appearance / Hygiene** - Do you smell bad and need a haircut?
- **Affect** - How do you come off to other people?
- **Friendliness** - Do other people find you approachable and nice?
- **Openness to Opinions** - Can you tolerate and respect differing opinions?
- **Theory of Mind** - Are you aware that other people have their own personal agendas?
- **Frustration Tolerance** - How quickly do you throw your laptop against the wall?
- **Sleep Hygiene** - Do you get enough sleep and limit the activities that prevent you from sleeping well?
- **Reading Fluency** - Can you read quickly enough to keep up in a class?
- **Written Expression** - Are you able to effectively write what you are thinking?
- **Oral Comprehension** - Do you have troubles understanding people when they give you long directions or complicated information?
- **Reading Comprehension** - Are you able to easily understand what you read?
- **Oral Expression** - Can you tell people what you know effectively?
- **Math Skills** - Can you use everyday math to solve problems?
- **Collaboration Skills** - Can you work in a group of people without pissing everyone off?
- **Self-Advocacy** - Can you stand up for yourself when you feel like you've been wronged?
- **Willingness to Ask for Help** - Do you know when you need help and are you able and willing to ask the right people to give you that help?
- **Procrastination** - Do you do other things to avoid doing tasks you don't like doing?

- **Study Skills** - Do you have strategies for learning new information in class?
- **Personal Interests** - What are the things that motivate you and engage you?
- **Anxiety** - Do you get nervous and fearful or avoidant about doing some tasks in school?
- **Mood Fluctuations** - Does your mood change your behavior frequently?
- **Purpose** - Why do you want to go to college?

Keep in mind, these aren't necessarily a question of like or dislike. Each has degrees and scales, and reflects your strengths and weaknesses. We are all great at some things we hate doing. We are often terrible at some things we love doing. Acknowledging where our motivation or lack of motivation lies is essential.

If you are great at math, but hate doing it, you'll need to generate the motivation and structure to work on something you just don't like doing. That may require finding the right time, place, or reward for doing it. Whereas if you love something that you are terrible at, you may require motivation and additional time to build the necessary skills to master it.

Here's the tricky thing with awareness: if you lack awareness, it's going to be difficult to be aware enough to know that you lack awareness. That's a tough one. Most people lack awareness in certain aspects of their life. Think of your buddy who thinks he is funny, despite your endless eye-rolling. His lack of awareness keeps him from recognizing both how unfunny he is, and how tolerant you are of his bad jokes.

Sometimes it takes a little help from a friend that sees you (and your jokes) with a little perspective. So, after reviewing this list on your own, ask someone (a teacher, parent, friend, or co-worker who you trust) to openly and honestly share their observations about you. Remember, these are your characteristics, try not to get defensive. Understanding them will be your way of owning them. Undeniably, knowing is a great deal less than half the battle; how you learn to take ownership of your characteristics will be the real challenge.

Regulation

Regulation is the ability to manage your emotions, impulses, and mood. Imagine that all of those characteristics you are now aware of are like controls in the cockpit of an airplane; while awareness is recognizing that you're moving at 250 mph at 30,000 feet, your ability to actually *pilot* the plane is regulation. Bluntly, just knowing that you lose your temper is worthless, unless you also work to control it.

College is a frustrating, distracting, exciting, terrifying place. In any given day, you will be required to navigate a range of emotions and address endless temptations. While some folks may help you with some of this, *if you are committed,* you are infinitely more effective at helping yourself. And, as you have proven to yourself many times in life, it's far easier to sidestep obstacles than commit to fixing them. Most folks do not have the energy or patience or desire to drive you to change. No one is going to remind you to eat when you are crabby or go to bed when you're tired and many of you left home to escape that external control. You must develop your self-regulation. This will be entirely up to you, and it's not easy. Keep in mind, almost one third of students who start college, don't make it to their second year[3] and even worse, only 35% of students with disabilities who start college actually graduate[4]. There's a range of reasons for that, but many students don't have the skills to manage their independence. Managing your independence takes effort and it comes easier to some than others.

Here is the truth of the matter and I'll save you the sugar coating: college is really fun and exciting, but much of it sucks. In fact, the part that sucks the most is balancing the fun stuff and the sucky stuff.

---

3   http://colleges.usnews.rankingsandreviews.com/best-colleges/rankings/national-universities/
     freshmen-least-most-likely-return
4   https://hechingerreport.org/vast-majority-students-disabilities-dont-get-college-degree/

Every night there will be something fun to do or at least something more fun to do than study or complete course work. There will be numerous nights that all of your friends will be heading off to do the most epic fun thing ever, and you'll be heading to the library to read about something you only need to know well enough to pass tomorrow's test. You will never need to know that subject again for the rest of your life. Less than half of your classes will be on topics directly relevant to your major, and half of those will be on topics or subjects you despise. Not only will you have to take those courses, but you'll likely have to skip the most epic *anything* to study for them. Take that in combination with cramped living spaces, poverty level lifestyle, a roommate who won't stop talking about Bob Marley, and you've got college.

For those of you still reading, please don't let this discourage you. (And, nice job regulating your distractedness!) Most people who finish college and start working actually wish they could go back and do college all over again. So, either life sucks more than college, or college is actually amazing if you do it right. I argue that it's the latter.

You have to strive — every day and every class — to find the appropriate work/life or study/fun balance. You will have to find ways to make sure that your study life supports your fun life and vice versa. You will need to guard against your fun life being detrimental to your study life and you will also need to be sure that you can manage your study life, so that you can have a great fun life. This is where your regulation skills will be essential for finding that balance.

Recently in the airport, there was a gentleman who was enraged with the fact that his flight had been cancelled. He was literally screaming at the airline employee and demanding that she right this wrong immediately. His veins were popping out of his forehead and he was shaking angrily. When the employee said, "sir, you need to calm down", he screamed back, "I am calm!" Forget regulation; this lovely man lacked cognitive awareness. Being aware of your mood and emotions will allow you to do something about them. Your first task will be to name the emotion and this will take some honesty, and modesty. Knowing whether you are scared, angry, anxious, upset, happy, frustrated, discouraged, or sad will help you to begin to develop strategies to deal with these emotions. However, without being able to name the emotion, you won't be able to own it. Often times when we are having strong feelings, it can be difficult in the moment to pinpoint the emotion. This emotional dysregulation itself may feel like the emotion.

For example, as you are walking toward class your heart begins to race, your palms get sweaty, and you feel like running in the opposite direction. You determine that class causes you to feel like running away. However, getting to the bottom of that dysregulation is the important part. Do you feel anxious about the social setting? Do you feel incompetent? Are you scared to see someone in the class? Are you so excited for the class that you can't handle it? Ultimately, the key will be to recognize those moments of emotional dysregulation and investigate them in more detail. So, what really is causing the escalated emotion, and how can you reasonably start addressing it?

Here is a strategy that may help you to stop freaking yourself out. In behavioral psychology, there is a practice known as functional behavioral analysis (FBA). The premise of an FBA is that all behavior serves a function, or reason, and by evaluating the function the behavior ceases. Imagine a preschooler who throws a temper tantrum just before noon every day. If we determine that the temper tantrum is caused by the child's hunger, we can avoid the temper tantrum by making sure the child has food. You can see where just addressing the behavior without the cause could be very problematic. If you gave the child a timeout instead of feeding them, you'd end up with a screaming hungry toddler in timeout, and then no one would enjoy their lunch. An FBA has practical implications for your own regulation, as long as you are self-aware enough to administer the strategy. Reader, recommit here – this gets a little complicated, but the concept will help you overcome some auto-generated but hobbling obstacles.

There are four components to an FBA: the setting event, the trigger, the behavior, and the consequence:

- The setting event is comprised of the events that are framing your day. Did you get enough sleep? Do you feel sick? Did you have a fight with your partner? Are you hungry? These conditions may contribute to the decisions and reactions you have throughout the day. If you haven't slept well, aren't you more likely to get frustrated with an assignment?
- The trigger is the event that incites an emotion-affected behavior.
- Obviously, the consequence is the outcome of your decision or behavior. For example, let's say you have a cold and didn't sleep well (setting event), you walk into class and find out there is a pop quiz (trigger), you immediately begin to get anxious and panic (behavior), and in your escalated state, you forget everything you know and get an F on the quiz (consequence).

Knowing how you are likely to react under a set of provocative circumstances and the consequences of your actions will help you to strategize to make "healthier" decisions in the moment. For example, if you wake up in the morning and realize that you didn't sleep well and have a cold, you put yourself on high alert that you may be more prone to anxiety, until you get a nap. Understanding this tendency helps you manage your anxiety in a healthy way. When you walk into class and find out there's a pop quiz, instead of panicking, you close your eyes and take twenty deep breaths. You continue to reassure yourself through positive talk that you can do this and that it's only a quiz. You ace the quiz and everyone in the class picks you up and puts you on their shoulders and chants your name. Or, more likely, you get a C and happily take it given the fact that you didn't sleep well and have a cold, but it sure beats an F. Regardless, breaking down these moments will help you to figure out how to react to stressors more effectively.

Emotional regulation is a process, not necessarily a skill. Most people have developed a set of strategies over their lifetime to help them regulate their emotions. It's more than just saying that you're calm, but *actively* employing skills to help you become calm. There has been significant research on the value of mindfulness practices, such as meditation and yoga, as well as the benefits of exercise in regulating emotional swings. You could read a hundred books on the topic (and I encourage you to do so), but I also recognize that someone telling you to exercise and be more mindful isn't going to necessarily do the trick. You need to do what works for you to help regulate your more extreme emotions.

Once you are able to identify your state of being, determine what works for you to help regulate that state. Then, use that strategy. If playing video games helps you reduce your anxiety or watching birds helps you improve your focus, then do those things. The key is to do *something*, though. If you are studying for an exam and just can't focus on the material, fall back on the strategies that help you focus and force yourself to do it. If taking a walk helps you to reduce anxiety, make yourself take a walk when you are becoming anxious. Remember, those moments of dysregulation are the times when creating positive and productive action is the most difficult, so be prepared to rely on those things that work for you and stick to them. Most importantly, begin to build a routine of the strategies that work for you. If you know that writing papers gets you easily frustrated, go on a long walk before you start writing, don't passively let it get to you. If you know that your anxiety makes participating in class difficult, how about playing some video games to relax an hour before class?

Finally, how do you get yourself to do things you don't like doing? That's pretty straightforward. Trick yourself.

Most people don't love working, that's why they get paid to do it. Unfortunately, you don't get paid for doing life. However, you can pay yourself. Most people, whether they know it or not, use some form of self-reinforcement. Your uncle probably calls it Happy Hour. It's the rewards we allow ourselves to have after completing tasks we don't want to do. Of course, your uncle could skip work and just go to Happy Hour, but do that enough times and there's no more money to pay for Happy Hour. Things go downhill quickly after that.

Balance your rewards with hard work, and do the work first. There are a million ways to do this, but you need to trick yourself enough to really believe you can't have the reward until you complete the task. For every hour you study, you take a ten-minute break with your phone. For each week you attend every class, you go to a movie. For every month that you exercise at least three times a week, you get a massage. Put your favorite snack on your desk in class, but don't eat it until you make it through the whole class. Or maybe eat half of it after you've focused for the first half of class. Know what motivates you and use that to get through the difficult tasks.

Expression

Everyone is weird. People who conform think people who don't are weird, and in turn, the nonconformists think those who conform are even weirder. People with tattoos probably think that people without tattoos are odd. And, at some point in history, someone wore a long bowtie and called it a necktie. So now all the necktie people think the bowtie people are strange, and vice versa. Nevertheless, the attribute that tattooed nonconformist bowtie wearing people all appreciate is *authenticity*. When you meet someone who is weird, but they own their weirdness and are comfortable in their own skin, they aren't weird anymore… they are unique. Rather than expressing awkwardness, they express their individuality. Individuality is always cooler than self-conscious awkwardness. The way we express ourselves is extremely personal. Self-expression is not who are trying to be, it is who we are. College, for many people, is their first opportunity to express their individuality in an environment where "peers" are the majority. And your peers are powerfully motivated to be open-minded. Instead of being confined by the conformist values of a small high school, college is a gathering of people who all march to different drummers.

We find ourselves investigating awareness again. Funny how that keeps coming up. But, ask yourself, who are you? How do you want to be perceived by others? Do you want to be weird or do you want to be unique? Do you want to blend in or do you want to stand out? Do you want to appear unapproachable or do you want to appear warm and open? Much of our expression is communicated through personal style. Our individuality is expressed through our values. Determine what you value first, and then dress and act the part second. Know that the shock value is mostly gone in college though. You could definitely show up to class with a purple mohawk and black lipstick, but if you act uncomfortable looking like a character from Mad Max, everyone will think you are weird. Whereas, if this is who you are, this expresses your values, and you can own it comfortably in your own skin, people will love you for it. This is not an endorsement for or against mohawks, this is encouragement to be yourself. To own who you are, but know that it will affect how others perceive you.

Having said that, most people in college have a few things in common: they are serious about their education, they want to be respected, and they want to be viewed as a responsible adult. Expressing these universal values along with your own unique style will help you fit in and be viewed more positively by others. Of course, you'll see a few people in every one of your classes wearing pajamas and looking like they haven't showered in a few days. The professor and the other students in class will likely take those people less seriously and quite frankly feel like they should grow up. Does that mean you need to wear a shirt and tie or a pant suit? No! This means you need to exude self-respect and express your individuality and your values.

If you're a hippie, then wear clean tie-dyes with your finest patchwork pants. If you are a punk, shine up the chains to accessorize your black skinny pants. If you are a tech geek, wear your best (non-offensive) sarcastic t-shirt about a coding joke that only the few folks as smart as you will understand. If you don't know what you are, wear what you would wear on a date or to church. Regardless, leave the pajamas at home, dress your values, and be your best self. People will notice you the way you want to be noticed.

Dynamic Determination

You've likely heard the concept of self-determination being thrown around at different points throughout your life. Self-determination is your ability to seek your destiny without influence or control from others. The concept suggests that you should have the right and freedom to make your own choices that might lead you to live the life of your dreams. Imagine poor Herbie from the classic Rudolph the Rednosed Reindeer cartoon (and if you haven't seen this classic, then you should definitely find it online before going to college!) All of Santa's elves thought he should make toys, but Herbie just wanted to be a dentist. We can all agree that Herbie should have the freedom to pursue dentistry, and that the elves of the North Pole should have access to quality dental care. You'd think that they could work out a compromise.

We all have friends who, running into a significant social obstacle have wallowed in self-pity. "I just want to be accepted for who I am... pout, moan, gripe!" Self-determination is not simply doing what you want to do in spite of what other people think. It's not just Herbie opening up his dental practice, but rather it's the ability to balance what you want to do with the information you collect from your experiences and those around you. Herbie could get together with Santa and the Elf Union to work out how to make sure that the toys get made, while also offering dental benefits to the other elves, which in turn fulfills his dream. You didn't expect discussion of elf-teeth when you opened this book, did you? Still, this is an illustration of a process called dynamic determination.

Of course, dynamic determination starts with your aspirations. What is it that you have always wanted to do? What do you love doing? What can you imagine doing every day for the rest of your life? Not everyone is born knowing they want to be a dentist or a firefighter. In fact, many people enter college having no idea what they want to do. This is totally fine, but more often than not, these people are contemplating what they want to do versus what they think other people want them to do.

For example, there are countless people who know they absolutely love to dance, but someone in their life has convinced them that they will never make a living being a dancer. This may be true and the information that they've gathered is that they are not good at dancing. Nevertheless, passion for dancing does not require actually dancing to earn money. There are plenty of roads that will allow someone to express their passion while still make a living. And, they can still dance every day. Even for those of you who always wanted to be something completely unrealistic (say, one of Santa's elves), there is still hope for you. The first step is knowing what you love; don't argue about reality just yet.

Once you have determined your passion, and yes, you have a passion, you need to explore everything about it. What can you do with it? What are the jobs that support this passion? What are the jobs related to this passion? Beyond actually dancing, a person passionate about dance could explore dance history, costume design, choreography, stage management, video production, dance journalism, or dance therapy. So, while Herbie the Elf could be a dentist, he could also by a dental hygienist, lab technician, dental care educator, administrative assistant in a dental office, a dental lobbyist in Washington DC, or he could make toys that teach children to brush their teeth.

When most people who want to act go to Hollywood, they take jobs that support actors. They hold lights, get water for directors, do makeup, act as stunt doubles or act in small productions. They are networking and improving their resumes. Very few of those people become stars, but most of those people find something that they are passionate about that is related to acting. This is the time and opportunity for you to explore all of your options and then determine what is your best direction.

This is where all of the previous skills we have discussed come together. You need to have the *awareness* to know enough to evaluate your best fit. You need to hone your ability for *regulation* enough to be honest about the emotional toll of a given career and whether you can handle it. You need to value your path and know that your eventual career will be aligned with your *expression*. If you are terrible at reading and writing, get bored easily, and hate wearing suits, then being a lawyer will probably be miserable for you. But pay attention to the Biggest Picture lesson. Maybe you aren't suited to being a trial attorney, but there may still be a career related to the law that will match your passion.

Let's return, for a moment, to significant folks in your life who tend to push *their* dreams for your life with a consistently heavy hand. For many of you, you are surrounded by people who have strong opinions, very strong opinions (and significant investment) about what you should do with your life, whether this is fueled by your parents' desire to get you out of their basement and keep you out of their basement for life, or someone who sees the talents that you don't. They possess incredibly useful information. Those folks will force you to take off your adolescent hat and ask some adult questions with an open mind.

Test your awareness! If your Dad thinks you should be a dentist, ask him to explain what talents he sees in you that would make you a good dentist. Not just saying that it's a good living. If your best friend absolutely thinks you should be a comic book artist, ask them to explain what they see in your art that they would pay for. If your teacher doesn't think you should be a video game designer, ask her what characteristics she thinks wouldn't be a good fit for that career.

Once you've exhausted exploring the intentions of those around you with strong opinions, move on to asking people who know you well without opinions. It's a simple question and you've probably heard it many times: What do you think I should be when I grow up and why? Use all of this information. In fact, you should write it down in a notebook, so you can deeply reconsider these beautiful nuggets and determine their relevance. Your ability to balance your dreams with the educated information of others and a dose of reality about yourself will ultimately lead you to successfully seek your true destiny. And if you are still undecided, you can always make toys, like Herbie the Elf.

In summary, as you spit your toothpaste into the sink and look up and see that beautiful "you" looking back, your journey of awareness (who you are) into your expression (who you want to be) stabilized with regulation (how you want to be), and directed at your dynamic determination (where do you want to be) begins. These four concepts work in conjunction at all times, with each informing the other. Your new best friend is now and forever yourself. Your journey through college will be as much about learning new things, as it will be coming to know yourself. In the words of Shakespeare, "to thine own self, be true."

Take-Aways:

- Don't be scared of owning who you are. You must embrace yourself and know yourself better than anyone to truly be successful.
- **Developing yourself requires perseverance, humility and courage.**
- Being aware of who you are, expressing who you want to be, regulating how you want to be perceived, and determining where you want to go will be an ongoing cyclical process throughout the rest of your life.

CHAPTER 3:

Turning Deficits into Character

"Your unique characteristics are what make you who you are
— strengths, insecurities, predispositions, the color of your
hair, and everything in between. Understanding how those
wonderful characteristics propel you and, also, hold you back
in the world is honestly the most important diagnosis you need
to understand."

I *remember the day perfectly. It was late March and one of those*
rare Vermont winter days, when the temperature had finally risen
above frigid and the sun poked through the clouds. As I walked to
school, I was splashing in puddles, hitting random objects with a stick
that I had found, and soaking in the glorious sun. When I turned
the corner and saw the red brick school, it looked like winter again
to me. Begrudgingly, I walked through the doors and saw my teacher

frowning at me. My shoes were wet. Apparently, this was a big deal. I thought it was awesome.

"You'll have to wear the classroom slippers and find a pair of socks, unless you can call your parents and have them bring you dry shoes and socks," she said.

That wasn't going to happen, seeing as my folks had reminded me not to get my shoes wet on the way to school. I put on the stupid slippers and baby blue socks. "You can't go out for recess; you don't have anything to wear on your feet."

Even as a 4th grader this confused me, because I was a smart kid. First, I showed up in wet shoes and socks, I couldn't get them wetter. And second, why would my teacher possibly want to keep me inside!? That always ended poorly for both of us. One of my friends said it was because she was masochistic, which at the time, I just figured meant she liked to be annoyed by 4th graders at all times. I wasn't too far off.

We started every day by journaling about what we did the day before. I was supposed to write about what I had learned in school, but I was always focused on what I would do after school. That day I began thinking about the woods next to my house. Every Spring they would flood and the downed trees would make for these amazing bridges. I had made it to the middle of the forest scurrying across trunks of trees when I came to a dead end. Not 30 feet away was a dry spot, like an island surrounded by water. It was the perfect place for a fort. I mean, we are talking Fantasy Island meets Blue Lagoon meets Gilligan's Island meets total 12-year-old bliss. I just couldn't reach it without walking through the muddy waters. And those muddy waters were, of course, mostly lava. I was out of luck... unless I could turn this abandoned barrel into a paddle boat, or possibly reconstruct several staves to make a bridge.

"Thomas, Thomas, Thomas, you need to write. We go over this every day, you need to write. Thomas!"

As I came to, I was staring out the window, deep in mechanical engineering La La Land. "Sorry, I'm just thinking about what I am going to write about."

"Why don't you write about what you learned yesterday? Every day I say the same thing and every day you just sit there and wah wah wah wah wah wah...." If I could hang a rope from this one branch it may be possible to swing across or a zip line. That's it! I'm going to make a goddamn zip line.

"Thomas! Are you listening to me?"

"Sorry, yes I was. Something about yesterday. Yeah, I'll start writing right now."

I started writing some bullcrap (my favorite word at the time). After writing time, we had social studies. I liked the concept of social studies. I liked National Geographic. I liked daydreaming about islands. I didn't like watching my teacher write dates and names on the chalkboard for an hour, and then telling me why things were important. In fact, I often felt that class disrupted my daydreaming and not the other way around. As she was going on about something that happened on an important date, I started looking at the globe that was sitting on the table next to my desk.

Worst. Placement. Ever. You might as well put a lava lamp with dancing hippos there instead, because I'd probably lose interest in that quicker. Anyway, there was this island I saw on the top of the globe called Wrangle Island. It was north of Russia; I had never heard of it before. Who could possibly live there? I had to know more... immediately.

As I began digging through the atlas that was sitting on the bookshelf across the room, I was interrupted once again with, "I didn't give you permission to get out of your seat. How many times do I need to wah wah wah wah...? You have to sit up here next to my desk for the rest of Social Studies."

Here is another thing that confused me, why didn't I just start in that desk every day? It would save a good ten minutes of the day and I usually didn't care where I sat. It was all the same to me. However, that day I minded because I couldn't see out the window. I was crawling out of my skin at that desk. The teacher babbled about another important date, the clock made this ever so slight tick at every second, and there were twenty-five more god-forsaken minutes left of social studies.

Back to the zip line. My dad had some wire in the garage that he had used for the raft last summer. I think it was long enough, but I wasn't sure if it was strong enough, as I stretched my arms out to imagine the length of the wire I heard, "Thomas! You are disrupting the entire class and I'm done with you. Go to the hall for the rest of class."

"But I wasn't doing anything. I was listening." (Okay, that was a lie)

"I'm not arguing with you, go to the hall."

This always pissed me off. I hated sitting in the hallway. It was embarrassing. Other teachers who really liked me would stop as they walked by and ask me what I did. I usually didn't have an answer, but I could always tell they were disappointed in me. I was disappointed in me. I wanted to be good and feel a sense of belonging in the class. But I always seemed to get in my own way.

As I was leaving the classroom at the end of the day, my teacher asked for my Assignment Notebook and began writing hurriedly into it. She told me that I needed to have my parents sign it and bring it back tomorrow.

As I walked out of school that day, I opened to the page where she had been writing, and read, "Thomas was absolutely obnoxious today. He won't be having recess for the week. Please call me if you would like more details."

That hurt. I wasn't trying to be obnoxious. In fact, I was doing everything in my power not to be obnoxious. Oh well, I had a zip line to build and an island to explore.

The next morning my Mom and Dad told me that they were going to drive me to school so they could talk to my teacher. As my friend Nate would say, this is called being up Shit Creek without a paddle. My parents were both educators, so they were often more involved than I had liked. As we sat down in the classroom for another round of painful talking and listening, my mom started the conversation.

"We understand that you had a rough day with Thomas yesterday. We know he has a hard time sitting through the entire day. We know he has a hard time staying on task. But if you ever call my son obnoxious again or treat him like he's obnoxious, the next meeting we will be having is with the principal."

I was listening, fully present, all ears, shocked.

"He is a straight-A student. He is adventurous. He is creative. He is curious. He has a lot of energy. He's a dreamer. But he is not obnoxious. We will not sit by and allow someone to frame him in that light. Is that clear?"

Please send her to the hallway. Please.

I was curious, creative, energetic, adventurous, and a dreamer. I was not obnoxious, hyperactive, noncompliant, troublemaker, or disruptive. Those were not my intentions; thus, I couldn't be those things. This was the first time a label had been attached to me and it was "obnoxious."

It didn't last a day before it was replaced by my actual characteristics. Replaced by my parents who knew me best. I drove them nuts (too), but they knew this wasn't my intention. Instead, they would open the back door and say "go play."

Or, my dad would set aside wood and materials he didn't need so I could use them for one of my many forts. My mom and I would make train sets, buy pets, and kept an aquarium. We'd go on camping trips to places that had waterfalls, and cross-country ski to the tops of mystical mountains. They'd listen to my ideas. They'd encourage my ideas. They knew my strengths. They were excited for the places I'd go.

It was from this home-grown foundation of strength, that I first began to understand myself. I knew the things I was good at, first and foremost. I knew I was bound for great things, not because I knew what they were, but because I was always passionate about big ideas. It was through reaching for these big ideas that I was able to contextualize those annoying little characteristics that would trip me up on my way.

I can't sit and listen to anything for more than about ten minutes without my mind wandering. I'm impatient and have a hard time waiting for anything. I am terrible at organizing things, especially long drawn-out tasks. I'm always late. I think of what I'm going to say next while someone is talking, rather than listening. I need extra help with math. My energy can overwhelm people. I like to make jokes, especially when I'm bored. But, that's just who I am and it makes me no less bound for great things.

It wasn't until college that I came to fully embrace my weaknesses, although I prefer to think of them as my challenges. Through a series of critical mistakes (e.g., thinking Zoology was about zoos and asking where Swahili was on the first day of my Swahili language class), but also great successes.

I began to understand how to adapt to a system that wasn't necessarily suited for me. I didn't focus on those challenges nor did I ignore them. I learned to work with them. I learned where I was best suited to study, adjusted my study habits, changed how I took notes in classes, developed organizational systems to help with long papers, and understood how to take care of myself. By acknowledging these challenges and actively seeking to work with them, I was able to let my strengths shine.

I built that zip line.

Not in 4th grade, but several years after I graduated college. It spanned 100 feet over a pond at our cottage in northern Vermont. It was glorious.

You'd climb about twenty feet into a tree and step out onto a platform where you'd grab the wooden handle crafted from a broken shovel, and swing out over the horizon as you streaked over the pond. It was surely one of my greatest successes in life.

Oh, and there were a few other accomplishments along the way — college degrees, a doctorate, college faculty, publishing a book, great wife, beautiful children — but not one of them was accomplished without dreaming and believing.

Thomas, *Ph.D., (41), Professor, Author*

So, what is a diverse learner? Let's start by taking a look at what the term "disability" implies. Technically, a disability is a condition that significantly impedes a person's major life function(s). Quite simply, if you only have one leg, it disables your ability to walk. If you are blind, it disables your ability to see. If you are anxious, it disables your ability to get a date to the prom. However, those one-legged blind folks who are anxiously trying to get a date right now are likely pulling money out of their wallet, ready to place a bet. They would argue that these are only characteristics that make it more difficult to operate in a world that values vision, stairs, and pretentious high school galas in a crepe-paper festooned gymnasium. They may have *different* characteristics, but they refuse to let those characteristics *handicap* them in the world.

People often conflate the term *handicap* and *disability*. Whereas a disability is a condition or set of characteristics, a handicap is when those characteristics are limited by a person's surroundings. Take for example a person who uses a wheelchair for mobility. Most people would agree that this is a disability. However, this person is only handicapped when they try to enter a building that only has stairs. If there was a ramp, this person's characteristics wouldn't prevent them from entering. Thus, their disability does not handicap their ability to enter the building. The question then becomes, is the problem the stairs or the person?

If someone who has a writing disability is forced to write an essay on the American Civil War, they are handicapped in their ability to legibly express their comprehension of the subject. Is the problem the writer or the assignment? This concept is known as contextual fit. Basically, do a person's characteristics enhance or inhibit their ability to be successful in a given environment?

If you ask a group of teachers to write a definition of disability, taking care to make sure their definition is as accurate as possible, an interesting phenomenon occurs. Quickly, the group divides into two sides: one side argues that the definition is too broad and the other side believes it is too specific. A broad definition labels too many people as having a disability. Thus, they begin to pathologize or diagnose people with diverse characteristics as disabled. Pathologize, in this context, means that a teacher looks at your characteristic and decides that it is an illness of some sort. Something to be cured or eliminated. For example, a definition of disability that incorporates anyone who has difficulty writing lends itself to pathologizing about half of school-aged children. A lot of kids have trouble writing for a lot of different reasons.

The other half of the group begins to make the argument that the definition needs to be more exclusive, limiting diagnosing differences to only the most challenging characteristics. Consequently, this precise definition often has the effect of invalidating people with significant challenges which prevent them from fully actualizing their potential. This exclusion may deny them the support and services they need to be successful. This group of illustrious teachers often end up ultimately arguing that either everyone has a disability or no one does. If the definition is too inclusive, everyone qualifies as having a disability. If it is too exclusive, no one qualifies as having a disability.

Think about it. They are both probably right.

It's opportunities like this where we get to sit back and realize the utter ridiculousness of arguing over whether someone does or does not have a disability. In either scenario, what doesn't change? The person. I call it mauve and you call it purple. That eggplant looks the same to me. You say it's a disability or I say it's a difference. It looks the same to the world. By nature, we are a group of diverse, mostly bald, mammals that are good at some things and horrible at others. As a society, we have determined what we value and sorted those differences by preference. At the end of the day, I think we can agree that we are all diverse learners in our own way.

If Drew Maxwell, the artist from our earlier story, was indoctrinated in a society where currency was accorded to the quality of one's art, he would have been championed the state's exemplar throughout each of his grades. So, the ability to understand our own strengths and use them in the most productive way, while at the same time doing our part to value differences and create a world that recognizes that everyone can and desires to contribute in their own unique way is the only way that we can finally settle this silly debate about who does or does not have a disability. Easy, huh?

Surely some of you with disabilities are thinking, "But when I went to the school psychologist, I played with puzzles and she asked me about my dreams and looked through the Diagnostic and Statistical Manual of Mental Disorders (DSM), she diagnosed me with a disability." Now there is absolutely nothing wrong with this concept. The DSM helps professionals to communicate about individual's characteristics in an incredibly broad and relatively unhelpful way.

In fact, that school psychologist didn't diagnose you with anything. They actually classified you. What's the difference? If you go to the doctor and say you're not feeling well, the doctor will begin to ask you a series of questions and conduct a series of tests:

"What hurts?"

"My throat."

"Does your stomach hurt?"

"No. Just my throat."

"Do you have a fever?"

"Yes."

"Do you have white spots in your throat?"

"No."

"Do you have a cough?"

"Yes."

"Are you a smoker?"

"No."

"What color is your phlegm?

"My what?"

"Your snot."

"Green and yellow."

"Does this hurt?"

"Yes. Why did you do that?"

"I diagnose you with bronchitis."

In this diagnosis, the doctor *deductively* narrows down your symptoms to a cause. You have an inflammation of the lining of your bronchial tubes caused by a respiratory infection. The symptoms led the doctor down the path to the cause of illness. The doctor gives you a few cough drops, some antibiotics, a note for your gym teacher, and sends you on your way.

The *inductive* process of classifying you with a DSM disorder is almost the opposite. Take for example the meeting with the psychiatrist:

"What did you do?"

"I punched him."

"Why?"

"I don't like him."

"Do you have a hard time paying attention in class?"

"What was your question?"

"Do you do impulsive…"

"No."

"Hmmm. Do you like lighting fires?"

"Yes, who doesn't?"

"Are you very afraid of anything?"

"Yes. Psychiatrists."

"What's this a picture of?"

"Me punching Billy for stealing my pencil...or a butterfly dropping a bomb on him. Can't tell."

"I classify you with conduct disorder, comorbid with ADHD."

In this classification, the shrink would prescribe you therapy, a smaller classroom, and a bottle of Adderall. This inductive process was looking to clump your symptoms together to name a cause, just the opposite of what the pediatrician did. Once the psychiatrist saw enough symptoms clustering into one socially constructed classification, they were able to suggest a cause. Let's be clear though, the cause of your symptoms is not a conduct disorder, the cause remains unknown. Furthermore, what if the psychologist also did some more investigation and found out your parents were in the middle of a nasty divorce, your brother recently died, and you were being bullied at school? You can imagine that the addition of these symptoms may lead to a classification of depression or anxiety. In one situation, the psychiatrist casts you as a bad kid who likes to punch people who needs meds and a straight jacket. The other situation frames you as a victim of difficult circumstances who needs empathy and attention.

What's the point? A classification, diagnosis, or disability is simply a generalization of your differences plus a fancy name. Your unique characteristics are what make you who you are—strengths, insecurities, predispositions, the color of your hair, and everything in between. Understanding how those wonderful characteristics propel you and, also, hold you back in the world is honestly the most important diagnosis you need to understand.

You must embrace you, even the parts you aren't particularly fond of. You must be as familiar with your own characteristics as you are with anything else in your world. You must be able to identify every one of your strengths and weaknesses, understand their impact on your daily life and adapt however you determine best suits your future. It's with this enlightenment that you will be able to see how you can contribute most successfully and meaningfully in this very diverse world.

Take-Aways:

- You are comprised of a unique set of characteristics that make you who you are.
- Just defining yourself by your disability will only limit your potential.
- Understand your strengths and weaknesses and use them to your advantage.

CHAPTER 4:

The Right College

"Where are you now, and where do you want to go?
Ultimately, you need to have a clear picture of what you would
like to gain from your college experience."

C ourtney could never decide what kind of ice cream she wanted.
It was almost painful to watch, especially in eateries that had an
infinite number of permutations. It drove me crazy, but it's also what
I love about her the most. She was unwilling to settle for vanilla, she
wanted flavor and it had to be perfect. In fact, on several occasions, I
witnessed her change her mind mid-scoop. As you can imagine, it was
no easier for her to pick the right college.

Fortunately and unfortunately, Courtney ended up in a college
town with five different schools after graduation. She decided to work
for a year to take some time to determine what college and what major
would be best for her before jumping in head first. She had a lot to

think about. All five institutions of higher education had their own flavor. Their own advantages and disadvantages.

There was Big University, which had thousands of majors and lots of opportunities, but overpopulated classes and layers of bureaucracy. Then there was Private College, which had small classes and lots of support, but fewer majors and not as much to do. Hippy College was full of alternative majors and flexible policies, but didn't have residence halls and most students were pretty weird. The next option was Religious College which was great at supporting their students and plenty of relevant majors, but you had to live on campus. Plus, there was the whole praying thing. Finally, there was Junior College, which provided lots of easy classes, but had few majors and lacked the positive regard for future job hunting.

So which college did she choose? All of them. Not kidding.

By the time Courtney got her bachelor's degree, she had attended every college, some longer than others. She first decided to go to Big University. It was the safest choice given the vast number of options and opportunities. She also was accepted to it, which wasn't easy, so she felt somewhat obliged to give it a go. Well, her first year was rough. She passed all of her classes, but never bought into the whole Big University ra-ra thing and felt completely lost on campus. She loved her roommates, but when they all decided to live in the dorms again for another year, she chose out.

Courtney transferred to Private College. It seemed to be the perfect choice if only because it was the opposite of Big University. Her credits all transferred, but her intended major, psychology, needed to be adjusted for the college, seeing it didn't offer a general psychology degree. Well, she was torn between psychology and English anyway, so she switched.

Coming into the school as a sophomore was a bit more challenging than she had anticipated. Lots of friendships had already formed among her classmates, and most people lived on campus. She had decided to live off campus. Things weren't easy that year. Several of her classes were very demanding, taught by professors who were extremely challenging, so her grades began to slip and she even had to drop a course to avoid failing it. When the Private College administrators began laying out remediation plans and requiring her to do more than what she wanted, she decided one year at Private College was more than enough.

The following year, Courtney decided to work and take classes at Junior College. She asked her adviser to give her a list of the classes that were most likely to transfer to other colleges and just took those. It was a smart move. Her classes were easy after Private College, and they were offered at times that accommodated her work schedule. This was the year for getting her confidence back up, and it certainly did. She was ready for college number four.

Courtney wasn't religious, but she loved the idea of Religious College. It seemed to be the warm, comforting place that she needed after a rocky start to her college career. The priest who gave her a tour assured her of the quality education, caring staff, and supportive campus. It was almost like she had walked through the pearly gates. Until, of course, she moved onto campus.

She quickly learned, surprisingly, that religious people attend religious colleges and have religious views. Most of those views were counter to her own beliefs. She passed all of her classes, and got out of there as fast as she could after one semester, returning to Junior College.

Cleverly, she had a plan — take the remaining courses that would easily transfer and then give Hippy College the (ahem) old college try. Courtney returned to Junior College, relieved but feeling a bit dejected. She filled out the application for Hippy College, which mostly required some sort of poetry and philosophizing about life, and was likely accepted before the application arrived, because, like, who are they to judge, man.

Courtney found her home. The classes were flexible and not overly challenging. The faculty was genuinely interested in developing relationships with students and she was able to pursue her desired major of psychology through a variety of alternative courses with fascinating practitioners.

She graduated from Hippy College with honors and probably learned more about herself from her collegiate musical chairs than she would have with any one college. More importantly, education was her ultimate goal, not a diploma from a specific college. Had she given up after Big University, she would have admittedly been unlikely to ever earn a degree. Rather, she was unwavering in her desire to find that perfect flavor of ice cream. When she did, it resulted in a fulfilling and diverse college experience. Also, a degree.

Courtney *(35), Teacher*

When most people imagine "college", they see large brick buildings with sprawling greens filled with circles of studying college students wearing sweatshirts brandishing their college name with pride. This image actually only captures a small portion of the colleges and universities across the country. College is basically the education you get after high school. The vast array of college opportunities is as diverse as the students applying to them. Picking the right college experience will be essential for your success. Most high school seniors and their parents do not realize that getting into the most prestigious college matters significantly less than excelling at your chosen college pathway. Employers and graduate schools will be more impressed with A's at "average" schools, than C's at the "best" schools. Even worse, failing out of school your freshman year will make the road ahead that much more difficult. You need to consider your college experience as a pathway to preparing yourself for a meaningful and independent life. Unlike high school, your options for what your college choice will look like are almost unlimited. You must be methodical and strategic in making this decision.

Think of college as a spectrum of options. On one end of the curve is the Ivy Leagues, the traditional, most prestigious and exclusive institutions.

These colleges are the most expensive and the most rigorous. Not only will you need to have near perfect grades, but you will also need to ace your SAT or ACT, be very active in your community, and possibly have a Senator for a mother and Supreme Court Justice for a father. Or, you know, the other way around.

These colleges will require intensive studying and the course materials, and the expectations and speed of courses will be extremely challenging. Additionally, these colleges make less exceptions and accommodations for diverse learners. They will expect you to do the work in the same way as your classmates. Not to mention, these colleges often have much larger class sizes. Finding individualized support may be more challenging than at other schools. If this is the experience that you are striving for, then by all means, go for it, but be prepared for it and know if it fits your expectations and abilities. For many of you, this probably sounds miserable. Don't worry, there is a huge range of options within the college continuum.

On the other end of the continuum are vocational or trade schools. These can be technical colleges and community colleges as well as beauty schools, medical assistance programs, mechanic and truck driving schools or other highly-specialized training. Most of these colleges offer certificates to show that you completed the necessary training. Some offer associate degrees, which are primarily two-year degrees. These programs are usually more specific to your interests and often less rigorous than a traditional bachelor's degree. Moreover, many of these programs are excellent primers to more rigorous programs and some even have guaranteed transfer programs to large universities, assuming you maintain a certain grade point average. More importantly, many of these smaller colleges and programs are equipped to deal with diverse learners and are likely to be more accommodating to your needs. With smaller class sizes and more direct access to professors and academic staff, you will have more people to access for support.

So how do you choose?

Where are you now, and where do you want to go? Ultimately, you need to have a clear picture of what you would like to gain from your college experience. If you know for sure that you want to be a teacher and believe you have the necessary potential to be one, then eventually you will need to complete a four-year bachelor's degree that leads to credentials and licensure. However, if you want to be the IT guy working at a company and sarcastically helping dumb people use computers, you may only need to complete a certificate program or associate's degree to be competitive in the workforce. If you have no idea what you want out of college or if it's even right for you, then spending some time figuring it out may be in your best interest. But a thing to remember is that very few people start their first day at Harvard "undecided".

Where are you now? For some of you, high school was easy, studying comes naturally, and you are ready to enroll in a four-year university and work toward your career goals. This is great information to have and you can begin browsing programs that meet your needs. However, for many of you, high school may have been a mix of gutterballs and strikes. You may only have a general idea of what you want to eventually do, but have no idea how to get there or are unsure you have the skills to be successful. In this case, jumping into a four-year commitment may be costly, stressful, and ultimately unproductive. If that is your situation, you'll need to be much more strategic about the path that you take to get where you want to go.

Let's assume you are unsure of exactly what to study and you are also unsure if you have the academic skills to do it. Before applying to and enrolling at a four-year college, many folks find it extremely valuable to enroll in a community college or technical school and take a few courses each semester. You could accomplish two major things with this route. First, you can complete some common prerequisites (courses that any college will require you to take, e.g., introductions to writing, math, science, etc.), get them out of the way and simultaneously, save a bundle of money. Second, you can experiment with some classes in subjects that you are interested in to explore your true desires and abilities. Many people who think they are interested in video game design learn quickly that they hate it when they realize that making video games takes an understanding of deep math (whatever that is) and a lot of coding, and isn't anything like actually playing video games, while other people find passions in courses, they thought they would hate. This will give you an opportunity to assess a field that matches your skills and desires. In contrast to a four-year college that will show you the door if you fail classes, most technical and community colleges allow you much more freedom to learn how to "do" college classes, while you're getting your feet on the ground, and also many provide much more hands-on assistance to struggling students. Obviously, failing a class isn't going to be ideal in any situation, but a technical or community college will generally be more forgiving while you are figuring out your path. After you have some experience under your belt, you will be more prepared and better suited to make a decision about your next steps. In fact, for many students, this route leads to much greater success in the long run and increases their chances of transferring to a college with tougher entrance requirements.

So, how do you do all this? How do you compare all the different flavors of programs and colleges? For starters, you can check out *The K&W Guide to Colleges for Students with Learning Differences* (15th ed.) for an exhaustive list of colleges that have a positive reputation for serving students with learning differences[5]. But then, it's up to you to do your own research. Here are some questions to think about and eventually to ask when you are looking at a school:

What is the average freshman class size, and who teaches those courses?

Most colleges offer smaller class sizes as you progress, but knowing the average freshman class size is hugely important. I'm not talking about the number of students enrolled at the college — I'm talking about how many students will be sitting with you, in cramped auditorium seating, throughout the required Freshman English 101 class. That might be 25 students, but at some large universities, this number could be in the

---

5   Wax, I. & Kravets, M. *The K&W Guide to Colleges for Students with Learning Differences.* Random House/Princeton Review. 2021.

hundreds. And, on top of that, the course is actually taught by a graduate student rather than a professor. This can be the worst-case scenario for students who need more support adjusting to college life. It doesn't matter if the eventual class size is 15 when you are senior if you can't get there successfully. This college may have your ideal program, but the challenges of getting to Senior year may be too great. This is another great reason it may make more sense to get your prerequisites out of the way at a smaller college and eventually transfer into your graduation college later.

What is your freshman retention rate?

Freshman retention rate is an excellent indicator of the quality of services and programs for incoming students. It is in a college's best interest to support their first-year students to be successful and most colleges focus on this issue. This is primarily a matter of recruiting appropriate applicants, enforcing prerequisites for harder courses and (hopefully) having services to support struggling students. Frequently, though, there is a disconnect between the admissions office and the academic services on campus. Thus, the admissions office may be under pressure to recruit students, but the campus is not prepared with the appropriate services for more than trivial exceptions. Fortunately for you, the proof is exposed in the retention rate.

The best colleges at managing retention, by focusing on appropriate programming, strict admissions criteria and academic and other support, have retention rates above 99%, but consider that, on average in American postsecondary education, if you start your freshman year with 1000 people, 333 (one-third of them!) will have said "sayonara" by year's end.[6]

What academic services do you offer? Any specialized programs for diverse learners?

Most colleges have an office or department called Academic Services. However, if you ask, "what academic services do you offer?" and they respond "we have an academic services office," be wary.

---

6   https://www.usnews.com/best-colleges/rankings/national-universities/freshmen-least-most-likely-return

In well-equipped colleges, Academic Services is the name for a variety of programs. Those might include career services, disability services, a writing center, a tutoring center, counseling services, mentorship programs, math tutoring, and the list could go on. A college's commitment to diverse learners and supporting their students is expressed through the variety of services that they offer. So, ask the question, and listen for specific answers that are relevant to you.

What does your disability services office offer? What is the average caseload size per counselor?

All schools will have some type of disability services office or someone on campus who supports students with disabilities. This is required by federal law. So just because a college claims to have a disability services office doesn't mean they are well-equipped to support diverse learners. Most colleges will assign each student with a disability to a services counselor. At some schools, these services are available to any student who needs more support. Other schools will require some documentation that you have a disability, such as an IEP from high school or psychological report, to access the services.

Your services counselor will be your first line of defense and best ally throughout college. They are essential to your success. However, depending on the campus, they may be worked to their limit. At some large colleges, each disability services counselor may have over 150 students on their caseload. Beyond trying to remember your name, how much is this person going to be able to support you effectively, especially at times when you most need it (which is likely going to be at the same time the other 149 people on their caseload also need their help)? Hopefully a call to the college Admissions Office can quickly answer how their disability services office can support you and whether their office has realistic caseloads to have the time to do it. Realistic caseloads might mean under 50 students.

How do students receive advising on campus and what is an adviser's average caseload?

Most small colleges require professors to serve as advisers to a group of students. This has some advantages and disadvantages. First, you are able to meet with an actual professor who knows the inside secrets to the college. That professor likely goes out drinking with the teacher who's going to give you a hard time. Maybe she can put in a good word regarding your character or intention and effort. Moreover, she is probably pretty smart and can help advise you on doing well in college. Ideally, you can develop a relationship and she'll be on your side throughout your college experience.

On the flipside, you may end up with either a brand-new professor who has no idea what they are doing, an old professor who should have retired twenty years ago, or someone who just doesn't think it is their job to give you advice. Then you might find yourself stuck meeting with an adviser whose advice you won't (or shouldn't) respect.

In contrast, larger colleges often have advising offices. These advising offices hire professional advisers to advise you. Now, in this case, you are starting with someone whose specific job is to advise you. Likely they have experience doing it, and hopefully got this job because they wanted to be in the position. Obviously, there are some significant advantages to this model. However, this adviser may lack the experience and insight into specific courses and majors that you might get with a professor, and they likely don't go out drinking with that difficult professor you're dealing with. In either scenario, the average caseload size will greatly impact their ability to serve you, whether they are a professor or a professional adviser. So be sure and find out not just who does the advising on campus, but how many students each adviser is seeing.

Do you offer counseling services on campus?

Many of you may not imagine that you will need access to counseling services on campus. That's totally fair, but it doesn't hurt to know what you have access to even if you never take advantage of them. College is a stressful time under the best of circumstances, and it's good to know what help is available if things get rough.

For those of you who know you will need counseling services, this will be a crucial question. College is a difficult time with lots of changes. Having someone dedicated and available to help you through this time can be the difference between success and failure. Not only will counselors be available to help you through these times, but they will also advocate for you if things take a turn for the worse. If the college doesn't offer these services, you can certainly access counseling off-campus. But a therapist unaffiliated with your school will have less power to help you directly on campus. Campus counseling will have the inside scoop on when and how to help you navigate college-specific troubles, like drop dates and incompletes.

Do you have a mentorship program for incoming freshman?

Many colleges offer mentorship programs for incoming freshman. These mentorship programs assign you an upperclassman to help you get adjusted to college life. Mentors won't necessarily walk you to class or take you to parties. But they will have some insight on campus that the professors and staff may not know, or share with you. A lot of information about your college won't be written down in a handbook or passed along by your adviser. Student mentors will have that information. They know what professors to avoid, good places to study, classes that are worth taking, good clubs and activities on campus, and other inside tips. There are a ton of them. Whether you like your mentor personally or not, they can be truly helpful in your first year.

How many classes do you require a full-time student to take? Can I go part time, if necessary?

Colleges have different rules on the numbers of credits or courses you need to take in a given semester or year. Each course is generally 3 credits and most colleges require you to take a minimum of 12 credits (four classes a semester) in order to be considered a "full time" student. This may sound sweet coming out of a high school curriculum, but four classes may be a bigger challenge than you're expecting. That's especially true if you have a couple of really difficult ones. Knowing that you have some flexibility to take a smaller course load will be helpful.

For example, some colleges will allow you to request taking 9 credits (three classes) for some semesters. You probably can't do that every semester, but if you know that Calculus is going to be pretty rough for you, it might be a good option to have a lighter course load. In fact, some colleges only require you to take a minimum number of classes per semester if you are living on campus. This is good information when planning the more challenging courses in your program.

Can I take courses before being admitted? What is your policy on transferring into your college?

Colleges have a variety of strange rules around taking classes before you have been accepted and transferring into the college. Some colleges allow you to take as many courses for credit as you desire prior to being officially accepted. Others won't allow you to take any courses, and may even make it difficult to transfer credits into the college. Even more confusing, some colleges allow you to take a set number of courses before being admitted, but then won't allow you to apply until you've completed a certain number of credit hours, and most of those will have be to be done elsewhere. For example, one large state college in the Midwest will allow you to take up to 18 credits before being admitted, but requires 30 credits to actually apply as a transfer student. You need to be aware of these rules, so that you can decide the best path to being admitted to that college.

Am I able to take courses in my major my Freshman year?

Colleges generally require all incoming students to fulfill "prerequisites." These are requirements within certain categories to fulfill your general education curriculum. These are courses that a college has determined to be the foundation of your education. You'll likely have to take several social studies, math, science, and language arts courses, even if your major has nothing to do with these classes. Some colleges may not allow you to take any courses in your major field until these prerequisites are completed.

Conversely, some colleges allow you to start with courses in your major to help you decide if this is the correct path. If your goal is college exploration, starting with courses in your major will likely make more sense than taking 19th Century Hungarian Politics (unless that's your major).

Am I able to take some classes Pass/Fail or Audit?

In most colleges, you can take a course as Pass/Fail or Audit. Pass/Fail generally means you need to earn at least a C to pass the course, which allows you considerable leniency in taking a course you are unsure about. Generally, this isn't the ideal way to earn your credits and many majors don't allow courses to be taken in this manner, but it's a good option if you otherwise might not take this particular class. Colleges vastly differ on this policy and the number of courses they will allow you to take Pass/Fail.

Your other option is auditing a course. If you audit a course, you won't receive a grade or credit, but it will allow you to sit in. This is a great option if you are truly unsure if the class will appeal to you or if the material is too difficult to pass the tests. In fact, auditing a course one semester and then taking it for credit the next semester, may help you get through really difficult courses. Again, you will need to understand each college's policy on this.

How many times can I take a class and fail?

It's obviously not the most comfortable question to ask, but it's definitely worth asking. Most colleges have a policy for how many times you can repeat a course and substitute the grade. For example, some colleges will allow you to retake a course up to three times and they will take your highest grade for your transcript. For those really difficult classes that may require more than one college try, this may be very helpful in the future.

Is there a residency requirement for students? What are the options? "Living and Learning" communities?

Colleges vary greatly on their rules for residency. Whereas some college require you to live on campus all four years, others don't even offer housing. Additionally, knowing the residential options will be important to understanding expectations. Many colleges have traditional two-person shared dorm rooms. Increasingly, colleges are offering four-person apartments or quads. You should know if you can request a specific roommate, how many roommates, and if you can request a single room.

Even more progressively, colleges are beginning to offer "living and learning" communities. These are specialized dorms that group students by interest area or certain characteristics. There are living and learning communities for athletes, engineers, environmentalists, gay/lesbian/transgendered students, people who need quiet living arrangements, foreign language immersion, and students who want to live with other people who are committed to sobriety. You should know if the college offers these living arrangements and the requirements for applying.

Do you have a summer transition program?

Many colleges offer a summer transition program for incoming and transferring students. This is your opportunity to ease into college life, learn the campus and begin meeting people. Some colleges offer a few days, and some offer a full summer transition program.

Showing up on the first day of classes in Fall will undoubtedly be difficult and overwhelming for everyone. But you should think about how much time you think you will need to transition successfully. Find a college that offers you that experience.

Here is who I am in a nutshell (fill in the blank); why do you think I will fit in and are there clubs or groups you think will match my interests?

Don't worry. This admissions person won't be the one deciding if you get accepted into the school, so be honest. It would be good to know that if you are an anime-loving nocturnalist who likes My Little Pony (you know who you are), that there is a Midnight Brony Anime Drawing Club every Thursday. This is a good opportunity for you to get a glimpse into the campus culture.

When can I come and tour?

Yes, you need to tour every college you are interested in attending. Admissions Staff are sales people. They are trying to sell you their college. You need to go and test drive it to see if the product matches the description. Kick the tires. Adjust the seats. Try out the stereo.

By simply walking around campus and observing students, you will quickly know if you can imagine yourself there. College catalogs and websites offer you one view of life at a school, but walking across the quad will tell you a lot about whether this place feels right.

Take-Aways:

- Don't fit yourself into a college, find a college that fits you.
- There is no "correct" path to a degree. Do what works for you.
- Ask lots of questions and use those answers wisely when making your decision.

CHAPTER 5:

No One is Going to Wake you Up

"College isn't the destination; it is the path to your destination.
Knowing how to navigate this path will be crucial for your
success and happiness in life."

Reality check: no one is going to wake you up. In fact, your parents are likely at home sipping Bloody Mary's discussing how nice it is to have turned your room into the guest room and how relaxing the mornings have become without having to pound on your door repeatedly. Similarly, no matter what any college tells you about their services, the truth of the matter is that you need to go to them to access those services — no one will come to you. Professors will not call you to find out why you missed class and your tutor isn't going to wait more than ten minutes for you to show up. Obviously, colleges and employees will vary on how intimately involved they are with your daily life, but you can't plan on someone carrying you on their back for the next four years. No one is going to wake you up.

Now that we have established your need for an alarm clock, this is also where you need to be aware enough to know what kind of college experience is right for you. Because, the good news is that there are plenty of specialized college support programs around the country that will wake you up. If you know that you will need help with learning independent living skills and a greater level of academic and social support than a traditional college offers, then you should spend your time investigating programs specifically designed for diverse learners, who require life skills assistance. Generally, these programs fall into three categories: college experiential programs, specialized college programs, and transitional programs.

College Experiential Programs are programs for students who do not have the academic capability of earning a full degree, but will benefit from taking some courses, getting involved on campus, and learning independent living skills. Colleges around the country offer programs like this and the price varies greatly. Often the costs can be offset through government subsidies, such as Medicare or social security disability insurance. So why would you spend money on going to college without earning a degree? Research clearly shows that students who participate in some form of post-secondary education have better job satisfaction and earn more money, than students who don't.[7] This is a great opportunity for students to mature and develop appropriate social skills. Plus, it's college and it's still fun. Many of these programs not only emphasize vocational and independent living skills, but also getting involved on campus. Check out www.thinkcollege.net for a comprehensive list of College Experiential programs across the country.

Specialized college programs focus on students with specific disabilities who have the academic potential to be successful in college, but need additional support. These on-campus programs provide students with a greater level of support in academics, social skills, and independent living.

7   Grigal, M., Hart, D., Smith, F. A., Domin, D., & Weir, C. (2016).

Not only do students have the opportunity to earn a traditional college degree, but in these programs, they also develop the skills to be successful in their career. Programs across the country specialize in helping students with autism, Asperger's syndrome, learning disabilities, anxiety, and ADHD. These programs are a great opportunity to be integrated onto a campus, while also receiving advanced support. Typically, specialized college programs charge additional fees on top of tuition, so they can be expensive. Additionally, your options will often be limited to that campus and the majors available at the college. Explore www.collegeautismnetwork.org for a list of some specialized college programs.

Transitional college programs have increased in popularity. These private programs work with colleges to help college-capable students develop the skills necessary to develop full independence to be successful in college. Programs generally work with students on improving executive functioning skills, academic skills, and vocational skills, while students practice living off-campus with varying levels of support. These programs are a great option for students who need additional time to transition and are still unsure of their college aspirations — or who might need someone to literally knock on their door. Given the supportive environment, students are able to ease through the transition to college and increase their likelihood of success, without having to commit to a specific college right after high school.

The continuum of college options — from specialized programs to community colleges to the Ivy League — should provide anyone with the desire and determination to attend college. Completing college isn't the destination; it is the path to your destination. Knowing how to navigate this path will be crucial for your success and happiness in life. You need to be realistic about which college experience is right for you and adjust course as you learn more about yourself. Regardless, know that there is something out there precisely for you, but finding it may be difficult.

Take-Aways:

- Seriously, no one is going to wake you up.
- Carefully consider what level of support you will need to be successful in college.

CHAPTER 6:

You and the Law

---

*"College is the full marathon and you need to cross that finish
line with very few exceptions on how you get there."*

O verall, I was doing great in college. I had registered at the Disability
Services office, but rarely relied on my accommodations. My
learning disability made it exceptionally difficult to write, but with
some additional time and hard work, I was able to work around
it. I would often drop off my accommodations letter at the end of
the first day of class, and then hope the professor wouldn't treat me
any differently. The writing center on campus was incredible and they
helped me level the playing field. Plus, I was going to school to be a
math major, so I just needed to get through the first two years and then
it was all math, all the time.

"Integrated Liberal Studies of Modern Art"... the words still send
shivers down my spine. At first, I thought it sounded exciting. Art

class in my high school always involved some form of finger painting and day dreaming, so I didn't realize that this course would be my new hell. When I told some friends, I was taking the course, their eyes immediately widened and their faces got pale. "That professor is undeniably the biggest asshole on campus." Great.

The course was mostly sitting and looking at pictures while the professor wrote on a chalkboard. Yes, a chalkboard that he would wheel into the class and cover the white board with; he announced that he didn't like technology. I surprised myself, and my friends, admitting I didn't hate the course. But truth be told, I wasn't getting a lot out of it either. Some artists were interesting to learn about and the integration of the historical context was actually pretty interesting, but mostly it just seemed like another college hoop to jump through.

Halfway through the semester, the professor announced the details for the midterm. "Three essay questions, no notes, 60 minutes." There are a few things in life I absolutely can't do. I can't juggle, I can't touch my toes, I can't hula hoop. In all three cases, I'm sure I could master each one of those if I really dedicated myself to those tasks. The one thing that I can't do, regardless of training and dedication is three essay questions, no notes, in 60 minutes.

I panicked at first. Then I remembered my accommodations and breathed a little easier. According to the disability services office, I should be able to get extended time and be able to take the test in their office. Not that this would make the task any easier, but it sure made it sound more doable.

After class, I stopped by the front of the class while the professor was erasing the chalkboard.

"Excuse me, Professor Asshole (I used his real name). I wanted to stop by and remind you about my testing accommodations."

"You're testing what-a-modations?"

Not a good sign. "Yeah, I brought you a letter at the beginning of the semester and it was from the disability services office and it explained that I have a (whispering) learning disability."

"You have a letter about what?"

"I have a (slightly louder) learning disability."

"So, what's your point?"

"I am allowed to take my exams with some extra time because I have some difficulties with writing and I am allowed to take the exam in the disability services office."

"Okay, first off. I'm not sure how you were admitted to this college if you can't write. Secondly, I'll be the one giving you permission for what you do in my class. I don't give extended time and you'll sit in class like everyone else and take the exam. Do you have any other questions?"

I could think of a few questions:

1. *"When Satan raised you, what scary stories did he read to you?"*

2. *"Have you ever killed anyone?"*

3. *"Were you passionate about hating teaching before or after you became a professor?"*

I decided it was best to leave it at "thank you" and go talk to the disability services office.

Well, this whole thing just blew up. I emailed my disability services person and they couldn't meet with me until Friday. On Friday, I was told she was sick, so I rescheduled for the following Wednesday. On Wednesday, when I went to her office and explained the situation, she first asked if I really needed the accommodation, seeing as I had yet to use it. Then she said, she'd contact the professor. Five days go by and two days before the exam, the disability services office tells me that I needed to have brought the professor the letter at the beginning of the semester. I did, but, of course, the professor said he had no recollection of it. How this even mattered is well beyond me. Whatever, I figured, I'll take the stupid exam in class.

One page. That's what I got out in one hour. Fricking unbelievable in my mind, like writing an entire trilogy for most people. I got the grade back with some excellent feedback: F. What a surprise. However, it just didn't seem to be right to me. The girl next to me who had perfect handwriting and to whom I thought was lacking in the intelligence arena, got an A. My guess was that she was going to hang it on her sorority communal refrigerator, so she could see it every time she made a smoothie. I was angry.

I wrote a letter to the professor, my disability services officer, and I cc'ed the dean of the college. I very clearly explained the situation, my frustration with the process, and contested the validity of the exam. I demanded I be allowed to retake the exam with the appropriate accommodations. Then I waited.

Three days later, I received an email from the dean saying she would like to speak with me and that I was encouraged to bring a disability advocate to represent my rights. Unfortunately, my mom was living two states away, if that's who she was referring to, and I doubt they wanted to deal with her. Plus, that would also mean that she would come for the weekend, make me cut my hair, and likely clean my well-nested room. I'm an adult now, I can represent myself. I began to build my defense and was glad I did my research.

Now I'm not the lawyer-up type. Ever since my neighbor sued my Dad for painting our house yellow (long story), I just thought suing people was for idiots who lived next door. Anyway, I did my research and I knew my rights. I would try to reason with the dean first and then I'd pull out the ace in my pocket.

The dean had a nice office with lots of faded student paintings from when she was an art professor. Ahhh, what great luck, another art professor. So, I explained my side of the story and the steps I had taken with the professor. I knew that most of what I was saying was falling on deaf ears. When I was finished, she began talking and explaining why I was wrong. I kept thinking, don't make me say it. She discussed the letter and the need for the letter and that this wasn't a reasonable accommodation given the relative ease of the assignment. Please don't make me say it. She explained how I would have had to register the exam with my disability services officer at least seven days prior to the exam. And that she supports the professor. That's it. I'm going to have to say it.

"Section 504 and the American with Disabilities Act of 1990 provides me the right as a qualified individual with a disability of receiving reasonable accommodations and to not be discriminated based on my disability to access the full benefits of participating in and benefiting from this government-financed institution, and furthermore I am entitled by my 14th Amendment rights to due process if I feel like these actions have adversely affected my life, liberty, or property." Slightly out of breath, I couldn't help but smirk a little bit. Take that, dean!

I was allowed to retake the exam in the quiet of the disability services office. I wrote three pages in 90 minutes, got a C, and was thrilled. I can't say that my actions propelled me to favorite student status in the course, but I had my pride knowing that what I received was—ultimately—fair. And, I didn't even have to sue anyone... just threaten due process, so only half as bad as my neighbor.

Steve *(25), Software Developer*

Understanding your legal rights in college is essential and it is even more essential for students with disabilities. Whether you have a disability or not, understanding the larger college paradigm will certainly be helpful. The biggest mistake new college freshman with disabilities commit is thinking that they are still under the umbrella of the Individuals with Disabilities Education Act (IDEA), the process which governed your Individualized Education Plan (IEP), if you had one, in high school. Unfortunately, IDEA expired the day you graduated high school, and you are now left to deal with Section 504 and the Americans with Disabilities Act.

What's the difference? It's like comparing the rules of baseball to kickball.

For one, IDEA sets up a separate education system with separate financing and different rules from general education. Imagine high school as a unique marathon where special education students get to set their own rules based on their needs. Some students could take as many days as they want to finish the marathon, others could use bikes, some could just run half of it, others could get piggyback rides, and some could just write about it. In the end, if the "special runner" met their goal, they would get a medal and a bottle of water, just like everyone else who finished the marathon. In an equitable world, this makes total sense. Set a goal and accomplish it. However, college is not designed to be an equitable world, and it is not the unique competition you may be accustomed to.

College is the full marathon and you need to cross that finish line with very few exceptions on how you get there. Maybe you'll have a little more time to get there, some more water breaks along the way, or some equipment to assist you a little bit. But those exceptions are going to be minimal, and the expectations are going to be much higher. Nevertheless, knowing the new rules, advanced planning, and sticking up for yourself, if necessary, will help you to that finish line ensuring that you are getting what is fair.

Let's do a little history lesson to set the stage; it will be brief but important. In 1953, the Supreme Court struck down the concept of "separate but equal" education in Brown vs. Board of Education. That ruling forbids school districts from segregating black humans from white humans. It set the precedent that state schools could no longer segregate public education based on race, but also paved the way for requiring public schools to serve all students, regardless of race, gender, or disability. The Supreme Court said schools should begin desegregating "with all deliberate speed." Seeing there are still segregated proms in some states, you can see that things moved slowly.

Congress passed Section 504 of the Rehabilitation Act that forbids public institutions from discriminating based on disability in 1973. That discrimination included denying students with disabilities access to public schools. In 1975, Congress passed what would eventually become

IDEA, to institutionalize the rules for educating students with disabilities. Finally, in 1990 the Americans with Disabilities Act (ADA) was passed that further clarified and demanded that public institutions provide reasonable accommodations for people with disabilities. Before 1990, a college could say they would happily admit students who use wheelchairs, but that unfortunately none of the buildings had ramps. The ADA initiated the inclusion of automatic doors, ramps, braille in elevators and wheelchair-accessible bathroom stalls. Slowly the world started to become more accessible and slightly more comfortable for everyone.

Now, colleges are required to follow the rules of Section 504 and ADA. In some extremely rare circumstances, if a college doesn't take any money from the government whatsoever, they can ignore some of the rules, but for the most part, all colleges take money from the government one way or another, so let's not dwell on it. These rules affect students in several ways: 1) definition of disability, 2) admissions criteria to college, 3) accommodations while in college, and 4) getting kicked out of college. Because these can seriously assist you navigating the tumult of this next chapter of your life, we'll explore each and discuss what you need to know.

Who Has a Disability?

According to Section 504, a person with a disability is any person who (A) has a physical or mental impairment which substantially limits one or more major life activities, (B) has a record of such an impairment, or (C) is regarded as having such an impairment. Major life activities include caring for one's self, walking, seeing, hearing, speaking, breathing, working, performing manual tasks, and learning[8].

This disability may include a permanent or temporary condition of deafness, blindness, an intellectual disability, partially or completely missing limbs or mobility impairments requiring the use of a wheelchair, autism, cancer, cerebral palsy, diabetes, epilepsy, HIV, multiple sclerosis, muscular dystrophy, major depressive disorder, bipolar disorder, post-

---

8   "Your Rights Under Section 504 of the Rehabilitation Act". DHHS.gov (June 2006 ed.)

traumatic stress disorder, obsessive compulsive disorder, and schizophrenia. Not to mention other mental or physical health conditions also may be disabilities, depending on what the individual's symptoms would be in the absence of "mitigating measures" (medication, therapy, assistive devices, or other means of restoring function), during an "active episode" of the condition (if the condition is episodic)[9].

Soooooooo, who has a disability? Apparently, everyone (or no one). However, a college is going to require you to provide good old-fashioned proof that you have a disability, which likely falls into one or more of the items on the exhaustive list above.

If you went to a public high school and received special education services or had a 504 plan, you are good to go. You'll need your file and paperwork from your high school documenting these services. However, if you went to a private school that didn't have "special education", but you have a documented disability from your psychologist, doctor, or psychiatrist, then you'll need all of that paperwork to show that you qualify as having a disability, i.e., psychological reports, testing, etc. Here's where it gets tricky. If you don't have any of those items, but believe that you have a disability, you will have some legwork to do. Why wouldn't you have these documents? Well, possibly your parents have always just said that you are different and that you need to work harder as you struggled through high school. Or, maybe you went to a really easy high school where your hyperactivity got you in lots of trouble, but you aced everything despite not being able to focus for more than ten minutes. Possibly your anxiety was totally manageable when you were in your parent's nest and the comforts of your fifty-person high school, but you are worried about potentially falling apart in college. In these situations, you need to get evaluated.

If you are still in high school, you can request, by law, an evaluation of your disability. However, most schools will likely deny your request because you've been doing somewhat okay in school. Your next option is

---

9   76 FR 16977". federalregister.gov. 2011.

to find a psychologist willing to conduct an evaluation. In this case, you can be up front with them about your concerns about attending college. The psychologist will provide you with a psychological report and likely make recommendations. This report can then be brought to the college to document your disability. Unfortunately, this will cost you a bit of money, unless your insurance covers it, but it will be worth it in the long run.

If after all of these processes you don't qualify as having a disability but are rather just a diverse learner, it is important to remember that almost everything from this book is still relevant. The difference is that you won't be protected by disability law and will not be entitled to accommodations. Don't worry. There's still plenty you can do.

Keep reading.

How Can They Reject You?

Section 504 states:

No otherwise qualified individual with a disability in the United States, as defined in section 705(20) of this title, shall, solely by reason of her or his disability, be excluded from the participation in, be denied the benefits of, or be subjected to discrimination under any program or activity receiving Federal financial assistance.

The key term for you to remember is "otherwise qualified." Simply put, this suggests that if you are qualified (i.e., they admit you to their college), a school can't discriminate based on your disability. Furthermore, they also can't simply reject you because of your disability. However, if your disability causes you to not be qualified according to their admissions criteria for all students then they can reject you.

Let's use a sports example. You want to play on a soccer team and the coach calls you before practice. She asks if you can kick the ball. You say "yes." And coach adds you to the roster. When you show up for the first practice, she finds out that you can kick the ball, but also that you only have one leg. The coach can't cut you as long as you can actually kick the ball (you are otherwise qualified).

Similarly, if in that phone call you say you can kick the ball and the coach finds out before putting you on the roster that you only have one leg, the coach can't reject you for your disability. Any rejection has to be based on the coach's requirements that you can kick the ball.

Here, the coach calls you and you say you can't kick the ball. When the coach doesn't add you to the team, you can't say she discriminated based on your disability — because you can't kick the ball (you weren't otherwise qualified).

For college admissions, the law is fairly clear that institutions can make their own decision about who to admit and who to reject. In fact, there have been numerous legal cases in which someone with a disability felt they were discriminated against because they weren't admitted to a college, and the courts sided with the college almost every time. Ultimately, as long as a college follows the same rules for everyone and can show they are making an objective decision based on the application, they have the freedom to determine who to accept. Thus, focusing on the application and the supporting materials will be extremely important.

Colleges are allowed to require students to take tests that show general aptitude and achievement, such as the SAT or ACT, as long as they require this of all students; these tests aren't designed to determine whether someone has a disability. The SAT and ACT are taken prior to applying for college and are not administered by the individual colleges. The good news is that both exams provide for accommodations if you can document your disability. These accommodations may be extended time, more frequent breaks, having it read out loud, or larger sized print. Generally, these accommodations can take months to get approved, so get on them early and know what accommodations you require.

Most of these "aptitude exams" actually do a pretty poor job at predicting college success. In fact, many colleges have done away with this requirement altogether and are instead asking for essays or portfolios. Regardless, for those colleges that still require entrance tests, a good portion of doing well on the exam is knowing how to take it. Therefore, taking the exam without studying or preparing is pointless. It is imperative that you enroll in an exam preparation course and/or buy the necessary exam guides and begin preparing at least six months prior to taking it.

Colleges are not allowed to ask you if you have a disability, nor are you required to divulge this information in the admissions process. Depending on the specific college, they may be actively trying to avoid recruiting students with disabilities and others may be actually looking for qualified students with disabilities. The Admissions Process is to determine your fit within the institution's future success, not judging your response to life's challenges. So, don't think you'll be the only person writing an inspirational story about overcoming their disability. Everyone overcomes something to get to college, especially when they are writing their college essay. Your "I had to walk four blocks slightly uphill to school and I got blisters" story may generate empathy but will not qualify you for admissions.

You need to determine if your disability is really part of your story. If it is not, don't write about it. Write about the reasons why you are attending college and why you as a person will benefit from it and how others will benefit from your eventual degree. If your disability is part of your story, then write about it, but not what you overcame, rather how your disability has expanded your perspective, enhanced your skills, or helped you to determine your path in life. A sob story will be put in the sob stories slush pile for when the admissions staff needs something boring to read. Say, when the insomnia is really bad and warm milk isn't cutting it. Then they'll grab an essay from the sob story pile, but definitely not when they are admitting students to their university.

If you get accepted, the college may, as a formality, ask you to divulge whether you have a disability. At this point it doesn't matter, so unless your college essay was titled "Me and My Disability" or you reflected on your successful adaptations regarding your autism spectrum disorder, they have no way of knowing. This is the time to begin setting up your services. They may require you to take a placement exam or provide other information to assist them in determining the services or courses you may need. It's best to begin asking questions early and understand the use of these assessments and what accommodations may be available for them. Ideally, these processes have good intentions and are meant to help colleges begin to help you as a student.

Maximize Your School Support

Public schools are required to screen students for disabilities and it is the responsibility of the school to identify and provide services for those students, a process oddly named "child find", as if it's a game of hide and go seek. The "child find" requirement does not apply to colleges. Thus, it is the responsibility of the student with a disability to identify him or herself to the college and apply for the appropriate services. The responsibility, therefore, is yours. Unfortunately, if you are a diverse learner without a documented disability, these services won't apply to you, but that doesn't mean you can't assemble your own special services in college, which could still be equally as valuable.

It is your responsibility to make an appointment with the disability services office. It is your responsibility to request and receive accommodations. And, it is your responsibility to give your letter to the professor on the first day of class. It is, also, your responsibility to use your accommodations.

Colleges are required to provide you with reasonable accommodations that do not create an unfair advantage, lower the standards or alter the program. Basically, they can help level the playing field, but if you can't write, they're not going to let you sing your way through writing class. With support of your disability services counselor, you should identify which accommodations make the most sense for you. Once you have documented these, it will be your responsibility to inform each professor of your accommodations and it will primarily be your responsibility to be sure you are receiving these accommodations. In most cases, if you request an accommodation after you've completed an assignment, the answer will be no. Be sure to advocate for yourself from the outset. You can always choose not to use your accommodations, but without them in place, it'll be difficult to justify them after the fact. And keep in mind, even without a sanctioned accommodation, you can always advocate for yourself based on what you need.

Most colleges have a fairly standard list of accommodations that are available to students with disabilities. There isn't necessarily a test that can be given to determine which accommodations you qualify for, but generally based on your disability characteristics you can suggest, or your disability services counselor can recommend, specific accommodations that will help level the playing field of your disability.

Which accommodations will be right for you? All of them… within reason. Obviously if you are not blind, you won't need braille, nor would you want it. But having as many accommodations in place from the beginning will allow you to see how your learning differences interact with your new college environment. You may not think you need an alternative setting for exams until you realize how terrifying it is to take an exam in a lecture hall of 100 people, while everyone is scribbling, sniffling, and every three minutes someone walks up to the front of the room with a disgusting grin on their face to turn in the exam. Like it was a race or something. Err on the side of needing more protection than less. Here is a list of the most common college accommodations, but keep in mind, you can recommend any accommodation you would like and the college will either approve it or reject it, and if you don't qualify for accommodations, it's worth understanding what may be helpful to you and advocate for it with the professor:

Common Challenges	Accommodation
Slow processing; anxiety; ADHD	Extended time
Slow processing; ADHD; written expression; fine motor skills; oral comprehension	Note taker

Oral comprehension; slow processing; ADHD	Recorded Lecture
Deaf/hearing impairment; visual impairment	Interpreter/Braille
Visual impairment; ADHD; sensory processing; hearing impairment; anxiety	Seating Location
Anxiety; social communication disorders; speech impairment; oral expression	Limited Participation
Anxiety/depression; health issues	Intermittent Attendance
Written expression; slow processing	Writing Scribe
Reading comprehension; visual impairment; slow processing;	Recorded textbook
Slow processing; anxiety; sensory processing; ADHD	Alternative Setting for Exams
Motor skills; anxiety	Service Animals
Anxiety/depression; health issues; slow processing	Flexible Deadlines
Obsessive compulsive disorder; anxiety; autism; vocal tics; health issues	Housing Accommodations

So, what do these accommodations look like?

- *Extended time:* on timed tasks, students can receive a predetermined amount of additional time. For example, students with disabilities may request time and a half on timed exams.

- *Note takers:* Many colleges offer this service regardless of disability, but for those that don't, you can request someone to take lecture notes in class. Often times, the professor will ask if there is someone in class willing to share their notes and they provide them to you either in coordination with that person or anonymously after class. If no one volunteers to be a note taker, the college will likely provide someone to do so.

- *Recorded lectures:* Most professors won't mind if you (audio) record their lecture, but if you don't have an accommodation, they can refuse it. (Recording video is more intrusive and therefore permitted less.)

- *Interpreters:* If you are deaf or blind or have another communication challenge, you can request an interpreter. This does not apply to requesting an interpreter for a professor who is difficult to understand, but wouldn't that be nice?

- *Seating location:* You may request a certain location in the room to be reserved for you. If you need to be up front to pay attention or in the back to avoid having a panic attack, you can request your seat to be located in a certain location.

- *Limited participation:* For those students who may have a difficult time participating in class due to their disability, you may request that you have limited participation. Generally, you would have to prove that you can't participate effectively to receive this accommodation. An example would be for someone with panic disorder to not have to give a speech in class, or someone with autism unable to contribute effectively to a group project.

- *Intermittent attendance:* Some disabilities such as depression, anxiety or other health disorders may make it difficult for a student to attend every class. Many courses have mandatory attendance, so having this accommodation would be necessary to avoid failing a class due to poor attendance. Generally, there is a process in place for notifying the professor and making up the work, but this accommodation is rarely given, especially in classes where attendance cannot be made up, e.g., classes with group work, science labs, etc.

- *Writing scribe:* If your disability makes it difficult to write in an efficient manner, you may request a writing scribe. This person would simply write or type what you wanted to say, but would not help you actually generate the content.
- *Recorded textbooks:* Most textbooks are now offered in both print and digital versions; thus, they are compatible with text to speech software. However, if audio version is not readily available, you may request that the college provide access to recorded texts.
- *Alternative setting for exams:* You may request a proctored exam outside of the classroom. This will allow you to take the exam in a quieter space with less distractions. You have to arrange this with the professor in advance.
- *Service animals*: If you have a helper monkey, you'll need an accommodation to bring it to class. If it's just a pet monkey, don't bother applying. But, still, that's a cool monkey.
- *Flexible deadlines:* If your disability prevents you from getting assignments done in a timely manner or if you want to be able to negotiate with a professor on the time you'll need based on the assignment, you can request flexible deadlines.
- *Housing accommodations:* If you have specific physical needs you can request housing to accommodate these, such as accessible accommodations. However, some colleges may also allow you to apply for a single room if your disability affects your ability to live with others.

They Can Dump You, Even If You Do Have a Disability

Did you know that colleges have the right to dismiss you if you do not follow the code of conduct or do not maintain the minimum GPA, regardless of your disability or diverse learning needs? In public high schools, if a student with a disability can prove that their misconduct was inherent to their disability, they can avoid traditional consequences. This does not apply to colleges, so follow the rules. Furthermore, unless you can prove that the college denied you reasonable accommodations and that this resulted in your failure, you can be dismissed for bad grades. In almost all court cases that have challenged colleges for a student being removed for bad grades, the court has questioned whether the student was actually qualified. Remember, the term "otherwise qualified individual" means that you are a capable of being successful in that institution with reasonable accommodations, so failing out may just prove you weren't qualified or didn't try hard enough.

Harsh, but true.

So, what do you do if you think your disability rights are being violated? Speak up. Every college will have a process for filing a grievance. However, start with your disability service counselor, they will usually advocate for you. If you don't believe they are helping you, ask to speak to a different counselor or the director. If you don't believe anyone is helping you, you can file a grievance with the college, but this should be a last result. In most cases, the academic service personnel are there to support you and will follow best practices. If you truly believe your rights have been violated and the college is not responding, you'll probably benefit from talking to an attorney who specializes in educational law to advise you. Keep in mind, at the college level, these laws favor the institution, so don't be surprised if you don't have a case. And at some point, a dead end is just the beginning of a new path.

Take-Aways:

- Know the rights and laws that protect you in college.
- The system for students with disabilities in college is very different from high school.
- Use your accommodations to level the playing field.

CHAPTER 7:

The College Landscape

"If you are properly advocating for yourself in college, it's almost inevitable that you'll eventually enter into at least one conflict that will need resolution."

The typical college landscape is much different than your traditional high school. For one, there is more than one building. Secondly, you don't have to take gym class, unless you sign up for it. Third, you can walk between classes without a hall pass and no one will stop you. Understanding how college is different than high school will be crucial for navigating this new super-sized bureaucracy. Knowing where to go to get your problems solved and who to ask will be extremely important. Plus, knowing your boss' boss is just good practice in life.

```
Board of
Directors/Regents
        |
President/Chancellor
        |
   +--------------------+--------------------+
   |                    |                    |
Dean of the School of  Dean of the School of  Dean of the School of
Education              Liberal Arts           Business
   |                    |                    |
Department Chairs      Department Chairs      Department Chairs
(Elementary,           (Philosophy, History,  (Finance, Marketing,
Secondary, Special)    Psychology)            Economics)
   |                    |                    |
Lecturers, Assistant   Lecturers, Assistant   Lecturers, Assistant
Professors, Associate  Professors, Associate  Professors, Associate
Professors             Professors             Professors
```

As you can see, a traditional college or university is led by a president, chancellor, or Supreme Leader (name depends on the state or if the Emperor is still around) and is made up of various schools or colleges. Each school within the college is directed by a dean. This will feel similar to a school district's superintendent rather than an individual high school's principal. For example, a college will likely have a School of Science and therefore a Dean of the School of Science. Within the School of Science, there would be various departments, such as the Biology or Chemistry Department. Each of those departments are run by Department Chairs who lead the professors who work in that Department. In smaller colleges, there may be only a few schools whose departments would be overseen by one or two deans.

Generally, the difference between a university and a college is that a university has graduate schools or colleges within it, and that a college just has departments. There are other differences, but most people don't know and don't care. I like to use the word college to refer to both because it's easier to spell and makes for a better sweatshirt,[10] and will use "college" to mean undergraduate schooling in general. Separately, there are a variety of "offices" that provide services to the college and students. These offices are led by directors who oversee staff. Let's go through each section of a college to determine who you need to know, who you need to love, and to clarify which folks you can safely ignore.

The President

The president or chancellor is like the CEO of the college. They help to set the vision and direction of the college and oversee the various deans. Above the college's President, providing support, funding gurus, and often some political cover, is the Board of Directors, sometimes referred to as the Board of Regents or Executive Board. Depending on whether the school is private or public, this board is either selected by the voters/politicians or is appointed by the president of the college. This board makes or approves the big decisions, such as tuition rates and expansion.

In most cases, the president will be somewhat out of reach for minor student issues, and you'll likely get a response from their secretary if you email the top dog. However, you should absolutely make an effort to meet the president. Why not? You are paying a small portion of their salary

---

10 See Animal House

and they didn't become president because they don't like college students. You'll likely get a brief ten-minute hello meeting, so be prepared to give a brief introduction about yourself and share your college aspirations. This brief meeting may come in handy later down the road. Don't ask for their autograph though, that would be weird.

The Dean

The president oversees the deans who direct the various colleges, schools, or departments. The deans lead their respective schools and oversee the department chairs and professors in those departments. The deans actually have a fair amount of power within their school. They help resolve conflicts, deal with professor performance, and ensure that the programs within their school are running effectively. The deans are in charge of hiring/firing professors, evaluating professors, creating new initiatives, and reporting to the president.

While you will likely have little, if any, interaction or need for the president's service, you may very well find yourself meeting with a dean at some point throughout your college experience. Therefore, it's probably best you request a meeting with them, before they request to meet with you. Ideally, you will want to meet with the dean of the school you are interested in receiving your major from. This is a great opportunity to introduce yourself, share more about your college ambitions, and potentially share more about your diverse learning needs. This is also a great time to ask them for any advice they might have for you. This will help to set up a positive relationship for you both down any future road, when you might need an administrator to be on your side.

The Department Chairs

Within each school or college, there are a variety of departments under the broader umbrella of the school. Thus, you can have a School of Math and a Department of Statistics, Department of Calculus, or a Department of Boring Math that No One Cares About. Each department is led by a Department Chair, who is a tenured professor who was elected or possibly drew the shortest straw to lead the department. The Department Chairs meet with their respective deans monthly to discuss strategies and regulations and whatever new initiative the dean is working on. Quite frankly, the Department Chair has little to no power, little to no authority, and won't likely get involved with any conflicts you may have within their department. Generally, you don't get paid more to be a Department Chair, rather you may teach one or two less classes than other people in the department. None of this is to say that a Department Chair isn't an important person to know, especially in your given major. They may be helpful in some situations and you will likely take one of their classes. They may have some power to make decisions about making exceptions for course substitutions or review applications for specific programs. They could be a great ally and can certainly bring ideas or issues to the whole department.

Professors

Professors are divided into several categories: full professor, associate professor, assistant professor and adjunct instructor/lecturer. The differentiation generally comes down to tenure status. Tenure is somewhat unique to colleges and one of academia's oldest traditions. It's also highly controversial. When a professor gets tenure, it means that the college cannot easily fire them. This job security is supposed to allow teachers the academic freedom to say or do what they believe is necessary to advance their field. Moreover, seeing that colleges are actually pretty political places, professors can be in opposition to the current ruling political party without having to worry about retaliation.

Where tenure gets a bad rap is when it's difficult to fire professors that are bad at their jobs or have stopped caring at some point. Unfortunately, every college has a few tenured professors that make everyone question the entire practice. You'll know who they are pretty quickly. Showing daily movies on VHS in their class (if you don't know what VHS is, you can look in a history book about technology from the 1980's) might be a sign. Or if they make an excuse about the copy machine being broken and thus, they don't have any overheads to display (more technology from the 1980's). A reliable clue might also be when they fall asleep in the middle of your presentation.

On the other hand, tenure also emboldens new ideas and gives professors the peace of mind to do their jobs the way they believe is best. It gives them the security to act in ways that are not necessarily politically advantageous. Some tenured professors are the best teachers at the college. Do your homework to learn who to avoid and who to take classes from at every opportunity.

For your purposes, the key differences are broken into two or possibly three categories. Professor, adjunct instructor, and occasionally professor emeritus. You'll see that there are gradations of professor. Some are simply listed as Professor. This usually means that they are tenured. It also means they are the most experienced instructors on campus. They've been around.

There will also be Assistant Professors and Associate Professors. These folks are on the tenure track (they are in line for tenure and long-term job security) but haven't been at the college as long as their Full Professor colleagues.

Professors of all varieties can advise you on your major, write letters of recommendation, and are generally going to be your major point of contact through your upper division (third year and beyond) classes. There will be good professors, bad professors, and professors that may be fantastic in their field without being a particularly good match for your learning style. However, they will have been at the college long enough that other students will know a bit about them. There will be a social network of information on what each professor is like. So, ask around.

There are also adjunct instructors or lecturers. These folks are faculty, who are not on the tenure track. That means they can't apply for tenure and are on a year-to-year contract. Often times, these are either people who hope to find a tenure track position, or they are professionals in the field who want to teach part time, because they like it, benefit from the professional association or simply need the money. Given the fact that adjunct professors make less money and often don't receive benefits, colleges often save money employing many of these part time faculty members to teach courses. In fact, in a lot of colleges you'll take far more courses with adjuncts during your first two years than you will with professors.

There is a constant struggle between professor unions and administrations to add more full-time faculty and hire less part time faculty. Professors would like to see more job security for their staff and colleges like to save the money by hiring part time faculty. Many small colleges have many more adjunct instructors than full time professors, and many community colleges only hire part time teachers. There is no convention on whether adjunct faculty are better or worse at teaching. In fact, many adjunct professors are also working in the field, and so they may bring more value to some courses than full time faculty members. And in some cases, adjuncts have so much more contact with students (they teach a lot of lower division classes) that they will be among the most approachable and effective teachers that you have. However, there are some practical differences that are important.

Adjunct instructors aren't professors. Professors see that job title as an important distinction, and they will make it pretty clear that you should know the difference too. The easiest thing to remember is to call the person teaching the class whatever they ask you to. That's probably Dr. Teacher-Dude. But it might be Ms. Teacher-Dude. Regardless of their status in the long-term college hiring strategy, though, these folks are your point of contact and the person grading your exams. So, that's good to remember.

Also, Adjuncts can't act as academic advisors and aren't the best source of recommendation letters later on. Because these instructors are on short term contracts, they don't have the political weight at a college that professors do. And every college is a political place.

The third possible distinction that you'll run into is Professor Emeritus. That's usually an established full professor who is in the process of retiring. They aren't quite gone from the university but usually only teach one or two courses in a year. These folks are often great teachers that aren't quite ready to give up the chalkboard (you aren't likely to see a lot of PowerPoint presentations in their classes), but it's also true that they are not a good choice for academic adviser. They may also not be really flexible in dealing with your accommodations. They worked out a teaching style in 1975 and why change a good thing?

Now that we have made the important though somewhat esoteric distinctions between who will be teaching you, let's just refer to all of them as "professors" to save ink. These professors are experts in their field first and teachers second. This is extremely important to understand.

Just because someone is the leading expert in the brain does not mean they will be good at teaching other people about it. In fact, someone who dedicates their entire life to understanding the mating habits of the Eastern Fox Snake may actually have already disqualified themselves from teaching anyone anything.

Colleges give little to no training in teaching and rely mostly on student feedback to judge teaching efficacy. In high school, teachers teach students. In college, professors teach content. Thus, don't expect professors to be great teachers for the masses, and certainly don't expect them to be prepared to teach diverse learners. It will be your job to advocate for yourself in each class you take.

Most professors are reasonable and most issues can be resolved with their support.

Establishing a professional, respectful and if possible, friendly and positive relationship with each of your professors is of the utmost importance. Some professors will actively seek to get to know the students in their class, whereas other professors may actively avoid it. Regardless, it is your job to be sure that they know you and know that you are serious about your education. Being upfront with them about your diverse learning needs will only help them to understand you and how they can help you in class. You should set up a meeting with them either before the course starts or the first week of class. This is a formal discussion, and best held one-on-one during their office hours. It's not for the five busy minutes directly after the first-class meeting, when they are trying to shove their notes and laptop into a briefcase without spilling their now-cold coffee. They won't remember anything about that meeting.

The objective for meeting with your instructor, will be for you to introduce yourself, share your college ambitions, and discuss your diverse learning needs. Ask the professor what they would recommend to do to be successful in their course. After the initial meeting, you will want to check in with the professor each month at a minimum, if not every other week.

Professors will have open office hours where you can stop in to meet with them, or you can make a special appointment. You should take advantage of this opportunity. Even if things are going well, you should be stopping in to ask two questions, 1) How am I doing? and 2) What can I do better? You should also review assignments and exams with them to help you understand how you can improve. You want your professor to be your ally in learning and this will only happen if you put forth the effort. If at the end of the semester your grade is on the fence between failing and passing, your relationship with them, or lack thereof, will be the tipping point.

The Saintly Secretaries

Now that we have discussed presidents and chancellors and boards and deans and professors and adjuncts, we can finally discuss undoubtedly and without argument the most important people at the college — the secretaries.

Really?

Yes, really!

Each department is assigned a head secretary or administrative assistant. Like the force of gravity in the universe, secretaries keep this world together. Without them, professors would be like lost sheep baaah-ing at one another while looking for their pastures. They would be inadvertently falling off cliffs or getting stuck in fences. Secretaries are the sheepdogs who hustle in back of the herd. Without fanfare, they keep the department priorities organized in tidy groups, or they can chase after the errant detail most expeditiously.

Department chairs act like they run the department, but everyone on campus knows that professors come and go. The secretaries are actually in charge. Secretaries know the secrets and shortcuts of every school. They can get things done faster and easier than any professor. They know about the top-secret forms that can be used to help you late enroll, early enroll, late withdraw, refund money from the snack machine, change your major, and probably even establish world peace and cold fusion.

Secretaries know what professors think that they know, but actually don't. They can help you get to what you need to know. The secretaries know all. You not only need to know the secretaries, but you need to love them. Flower them with affection and respect. Volunteer to help them or just sit in their office and bat your puppy dog eyes at them. Say hello to them every day that you see them. And if you don't see them, go find them and say hello. They will be your biggest ally and can help you when no one else can. No kidding. Seriously. A college's administrative assistant staff—the secretaries—may be the single most important people to know in your college experience.

Resolving Conflicts Up the Food Chain

If you are properly advocating for yourself in college, it's almost inevitable that you'll eventually enter into at least one conflict that will need resolution. That's not to say you will be picking fights. It's just the case that you'll need to insist on looking out for your particular needs. The college isn't always going to see those on its own.

Understanding the power hierarchy will be essential for properly resolving these conflicts. Generally, the rule is to be professional and kill them with kindness. Angry chest-beating and empty threats will lead you quickly down a dead end. For the most part, college faculty and staff want you to succeed. Appealing to their better angels and providing reasonable arguments will likely increase your chances of success.

Because most conflicts will be generated at the classroom level, you will need to air your initial concerns with your professor. However, seeing that your professor is likely the cause of the conflict, being unable to resolve it directly with them will likely require that you move your complaint up the chain of command. As I mentioned, department chairs will generally stay out of conflicts, although they may be willing to help mediate. That's especially true if they know you from around the office. You've met with them, and always seem to be helping out the administrative assistants, right?

If this isn't something the department chair mediates, you'll need to take your complaint to the Dean. They have the authority to rule in your favor. Keep in mind, this isn't for trivial issues, like you don't care for your professor's cologne or a slight disagreement regarding one question on an exam. Deans are for the big things that you and your trusted allies have deemed to be unfair or inappropriate.

When do you get the dean involved? As a last resort *and* when you and some smart people around you believe that you have a valid concern or complaint. So, run it by other (employed) people you work with at the college, like your mentor, adviser, disability services counselor, or even one of the secretaries, first. Valid concerns could be over an excused, or unexcused, absence that affected your grade. Maybe over a requirement to do something in class that is incompatible with your accommodation plan, or a grade on an exam or assignment that you believe was unfairly given.

Remember that college is the greatest Young Adult training mechanism in the world. This is one of those difficult lessons to practice, excepting only questions of legal rights, you must always attempt to work out everything you can with your professor first. Let the professor know that you are in disagreement with them. If you intend to take your grievance up the food chain you should first let your professor know that you will be taking your disagreement to the dean. This will not only allow them to think twice about their decision, but also it is professional to let them know first that you are considering contesting their "last word."

Now, after you sincerely engaged with the professor and couldn't resolve it, you have a Wild Card. You can appeal. You have **one**, maybe **two** opportunities in your entire college career to involve the dean. Any more than that and no one will take you seriously anymore. If you are going to use your Wild Card by involving the dean, then draft a well-written email that outlines your specific concerns with evidence to support your complaint. Attach any relevant evidence, such as any email correspondence or scans of the assignment in question, notes from discussions with your professor and other school employees. Then send it to the dean and "cc" the professor. If you need help with this process, work with your trusted support team — angry or incoherent emails will not get you closer to your goal. You simply need to lay out the facts and request a meeting.

At this point, the dean will immediately get in touch with the professor and hear their side of the story, and let's face it, probably talk smack on you. If, in the end, the dean sides with the professor, you will likely get a polite "thanks, but no thanks" response and this may be the end of your complaint. You may just need to live with it. However, if the dean does have some questions with how the situation was handled, they may hear you out or be willing to create a plea deal at your meeting.

At the meeting, dress up and be professional. Explain your situation rationally, and as best as you can, without being overly emotional. Deans aren't generally moved by tears. Describe what outcome you would like to see. It's likely that the professor will be invited to the meeting, so don't feel intimidated, this is purely business. If they offer you a plea deal like, "I won't let you retake the exam, but you can do a follow up essay for extra credit," take it, follow through on it, and do it well.

The dean will never listen to you again if you don't follow through. If you do not get what you want at the meeting, you should end the meeting cordially and thank everyone for considering your request.

If your complaint was denied, you will then need to decide if this is the hill you want to die on, or basically, are you really right and is it truly worth your energy? If you decide that it's not worth pursuing, send a follow up email to the dean and your professor thanking them for the time and letting them know how you might change in the future, i.e. I'll study harder, I'll go to the writing center, etc.

If you disagree and want to continue to pursue your complaint, you'll likely be taking your argument to the president, so you'll want to consult with an advocate or educational attorney. However, let's not get too worked up here, this will likely never happen, so don't start searching for an attorney now.

Take-Aways:

- Be familiar with the bureaucratic structure in college and use it to your advantage.
- Addressing and resolving conflicts is simply advocating for your rights.
- Secretaries are the real power at your college. Know them. Love them.

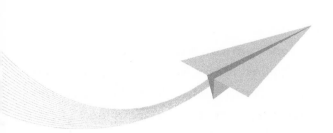

CHAPTER 8:

The Right Courses

"In blunter terms, sleeping through classes is a stupid waste of time and tuition so choose the schedule that will increase your chances for success."

Unlike high school, in college you have many options for courses. You have to earn a certain number of credits to graduate and you have to satisfy requirements in subjects you may not really want to study, but there are a lot of choices. Generally, you will have to earn 120 credits before you can graduate. There are two types of courses that you will be required to take, prerequisites ("pre-reqs", as the cool kids call them) and courses in your major. Roughly half of your courses will be prerequisites and the other half will be in your major.

In most colleges, your first two years of college will be devoted to satisfying your prerequisites. Prerequisite courses are a sampling of courses from a variety of subjects that provide you with a liberal studies background or basically the foundation for your major. You will likely have some choice over your specific pre-reqs in each subject.

For example, you may be required to take two courses in the History department, but you can choose between ten different history courses. This will allow you to not only take courses that may be of more interest to you, but more importantly, allow you to also select courses that are less difficult and/or taught by good professors. Obviously, choosing a course that interests you is the most important first step, however, if you learn that this course is extremely difficult and taught by a professor who everyone says to avoid, you may think twice.

Unfortunately, pre-reqs can be frustrating. There will be a handful of courses where you will ask the question every day, "how is this relevant to my life and my future career?" College involves a lot of jumping through hoops, and pre-reqs require the most hoop-jumping. As you are sitting through Molecular Biology when you hope to be an English major or sitting through 17th Century Poetry when you hope to be a biology major, you will need to remind yourself that you are getting smarter. Just grin and bear it. On the bright side, maybe you'll find some good dinner party conversation lines in these classes like, "Do you prefer cellular translation or transcription?" or "I think Jonathan Swift was way ahead of his time: 'Such gaudy tulips raised from dung', I mean who says that?"

You have probably already heard this daunting question a million times, "What are you going to major in?" It's no different than saying to someone, "So what do you want to do for the rest of your life?" Very few people can answer that question in their teens. College is actually a good place to start deciding where your path will begin.

There are some advantages to knowing what you would like to major in when you start college, but being undecided is completely fine. Sampling a variety of courses and spending some time really deliberating about what you would like to major in will be extremely helpful. In fact, many people are positive about what they would like to major in when they start college, but either decide they hate it or find something else they love more. This is the beauty of your first two years of college, you have time to decide and time to change your mind.

If you are undecided, think of the types of jobs you may be interested in doing someday and then ask your adviser what majors make the most sense for that job. Then take some classes in that topic and see if you like it. As long as they are satisfying some pre-reqs, you are moving in the right direction.

If you do know what you want to major in, then you have some distinct advantages. As we discussed, about half of your courses will be pre-reqs and the other half will be in your major. However, many of the courses in your major will also be courses that satisfy your pre-reqs. This will allow you to double dip.

You should work with your adviser and study the courses you need for your pre-req and major and decide which courses can satisfy both. For example, if you are going to be a Computer Science Major which requires you to take History of Computer Science, remember that History of Computer Science also satisfies a pre-req in History. You've effectively double dipped. Score! There will be plenty of opportunities for this, so be on the lookout for double dips.

If you are still having trouble deciding what your major will be as you progress through college, there are still options. That might be especially true if you are thinking about graduate school. If some kind of graduate school is in your future, then you can elect a general track without worrying about needing your major to immediately qualify you for a particular a job. For example, if you know you want to do some kind of work with people, major in psychology. If you know you want to do something with math, major in mathematics. Graduate school will be an opportunity to focus on specific areas related to your bachelor's degree, like social work or accounting.

Finally, if you don't consider grad school as your next step, you can always fall back on a Liberal Arts degree. Most colleges have some type of liberal arts degree and though they vary in name, a Liberal Arts degree is not much different than the diploma you earned in high school. You will take a broad spectrum of courses in many different disciplines and acquire a general bachelor's degree. This degree will still give you some flexibility if you are considering graduate school and will give you the college graduate diploma advantage when applying for work.

Most colleges will require you to take a minimum of four courses or 12 credits each semester. However, like everything in college, there are exceptions to this rule. If you are concerned about the rigor of managing four courses in your first year, you can request a reduced load, especially if you have a documented disability. There is no shame in this and you can easily get back on track later. Starting on the right foot will be essential, so overwhelming yourself and taking a full load your first semester may not be wise. Consider taking three courses in your first semester, or at the very least, make sure your fourth one is something easy like Underwater Basket Weaving 101 (although that doesn't sound too simple). This will allow you to learn the ropes and really focus on learning how to be successful in college. If you do well your first semester, then take four courses the following semester. If you struggled, then take three courses again the following semester. You can easily catch up by taking one or two courses in the summer.

Choosing your course schedule will be almost as important as choosing the right classes. This is pretty simple. If you are not a morning person, don't take morning classes. If you get sleepy by the end of the day, don't take evening classes. There is no shortage of college students who sleep through their 7:00 AM classes every day or miss them altogether. Not only is this an extremely expensive nap, but it was unnecessary. In blunter terms, sleeping through classes is a stupid waste of time and tuition so choose the schedule that will increase your chances for success.

If you get overwhelmed easily, spread your courses throughout the week more. If you like to get down and dirty, schedule them all on two days. Regardless, you have control over not only what classes you take, but also when you take them. Obviously, there may be times when your options are limited and you have to take a course at a time that you would rather be sleeping, but at least they will be few and far between with some thoughtful preparation.

Unlike high school, colleges offer the opportunity to take courses without worrying about a letter grade. Auditing a course allows you to basically listen in and participate in the course, without being graded, but you won't receive credit for the course. This is a great opportunity to "try out" a course before actually taking it. This may seem like a tremendous waste of your time, but taking a course that is too difficult or too boring and failing it is a significantly larger waste of time AND money. If you are unsure of whether a course is right for you, consider auditing it first and then signing up for it the following semester. Or, you know, forever avoiding it.

Another option is to take a course Pass/Fail. This will allow you to meet the minimum requirements to receive the credit for the course without the need to worry about a specific letter grade. Colleges have specific conditions for taking a course pass/fail and usually only allow a limited number of courses to be taken this way. Nevertheless, if there is a course that you are concerned will be extremely difficult and they allow it to be graded pass/fail, this may be a great option for taking some of the pressure off. Given that you may only be able to take a few classes this way, be extremely selective in choosing which courses.

Additionally, some colleges will allow you to change the status up until a certain point. So, if you are taking a course for a letter grade and you begin to struggle, the college may allow you to switch to pass/fail with the blessing of your professor. You may also be able to start a class pass/fail and if you are excelling, switch it to a letter grade format, but be sure you confirm these options before registering.

Take-Aways:

- Carefully and strategically select the courses you are going to take each semester.

- Be realistic about the types of classes you are going to take, the number of courses, and how you choose to take them.
- Choose not only the best classes for you, but also the best *time* to take them.

CHAPTER 9:

The College Classroom

"But seriously — be sure to read the syllabus. Know the
syllabus. Be the syllabus."

---

*I*t was likely the most boring class I have ever taken, Chemistry
101. The only upside of the course was that I was taking it with
my college roommate, so we forced one another out of bed at 7:00 am
to walk to the class together. Then, we could work on the crossword
puzzle together during class. Otherwise, we probably would never had
made it.

The class was held in a large drab lecture hall with at least 200
other uninspired crossword solvers who were trying to stay awake. The
professor was the exact opposite of Bill Nye the Science Guy and likely
had a fetish for torturing people with his slow words and monotone
voice. He'd spend the entire class facing the large chalkboard writing
out chemical equations with his only button-down shirt from 1950

untucked from his pleated khaki pants that piled on top of his Velcro generic white tennis shoes. He'd talk to the chalkboard and we thought occasionally he would fall asleep while standing.

Taking this class was the result of one-part bad planning and two parts bad luck. The other section of chemistry was taught by Dr. Slamiri, or Dr. Slam as he liked to be called. He had a television show on PBS and would often be seen riding around campus on his moped high fiving all 200 of this semester's students whose name and favorite ice cream flavor he took the time to learn. He would start every class with an experiment to introduce the lesson of the day. His eager students never knew exactly what experiment to expect but there were rumors of anti-gravity, neutron bombs, love potions, and pigs flying. In order to get into his class, like popular concert tickets, you had to register early before it filled up. We didn't get the message and thus, were stuck with the chemistry zombie drooling equations at us.

What struck us was that both sections used the same text books, same tests, same assignments, and had the same grading policy. It was just that our course was being delivered in a poop truck and the other section was being delivered by a wizard on a dragon riding a unicorn. We struggled to learn every day, while our friends in Dr. Slam's class were all changing majors to chemistry. It just didn't seem fair.

And then one day, when all of the stars had apparently aligned and the moon was full, our zombie professor announced that we would start class with a demonstration. Slowly students began looking up in shock from their crossword puzzles with some slight fear that this demonstration may simply involve writing faster on the chalkboard, to discover some equipment set up on the front table.

"It has come to my attention through some unsolicited feedback that you may be interested in having some more demonstrations in class to aid in your learning. So today I will be demonstrating the reaction of expansion through an ice bomb."

My roommate turned to me and said, "Did he say ice bomb? I think he said ice bomb?"

The professor then mumbled something about something. We only heard ice bomb. He held up a metal mortar with a screw top the size of a large grenade and filled it with water. He then placed it in a plastic bin and said something else, again we only heard ice bomb. He poured liquid nitrogen over the top of it and we all put our hands over our heads. Was this his way of ending our misery? We all waited and waited, and then we heard a little sizzle and a pop and the metal casing on the ice bomb split into two.

"Well, I guess something went wrong. Anyway, let me write out what should have happened on the chalkboard."

And back he went to slowly torturing us again. The disappointment in the room was palpable. It was like someone said, "watch as I pull a rabbit out of my hat, nothing up my sleeves" and then proceeded to pull out a small piece of rabbit fur. We just couldn't accept the lost potential of the ice bomb.

So, the next class, we sat up front with a plan. As the professor walked out from behind his hypnotizingly-dull chalkboard, we began to chant in a whisper "ice bomb, ice bomb, ice bomb." As the people around us began to join in on the chant, the professor tried to silence us.

"Now students, please stop chanting and pull out your notebooks, there will be no ice bomb today." But it only emboldened us, the whole class began chanting, "ICE BOMB, ICE BOMB, ICE BOMB!" We weren't going to take no for an answer. Eventually, he yelled, "Fine, we'll try the ice bomb again," as he walked out of his class back to his lair.

He came back with all of the necessary equipment about ten minutes later and slowly set it up as a hush fell across the class. He mumbled something something "ice bomb" something.

He poured water into the mortar, "ice bomb."

He screwed the top down, "ice bomb"

He set it into the plastic bin, "ice bomb".

And as he prepared to pour the liquid nitrogen onto the mortar, the class resumed the chant, "ICE BOMB, ICE BOMB, ICE BOMB".

He doused the mortar and after a brief pause, the ice bomb exploded with such force that water sprayed across the front row and hit the 20-foot ceiling, as he tumbled over backwards and landed against the chalkboard.

After a brief silence from the stunned class, everyone leaped to their feet with a thunderous applause and shouts of "ICE BOMB!".

From that day forward, we sat in the front row and when he'd come out to teach, if we didn't see a demonstration set up, we'd look at him and quietly chant "ice bomb, ice bomb, ice bomb" until he'd quickly think of something to appease us. By the end of the semester, he was doing a demonstration each class and although he'd quickly resume his chalkboard mumbling after the day's experiment giddiness settled, we successfully got him to teach us something.

Although I got a C in the class, it had gone from my least favorite class, to my second least favorite class. A victory, nonetheless.

John *(41), Small Business Owner*

Teaching vs. Learning

Tragically, most people, even veteran teachers, can't describe the difference between teaching and learning. It is probably the most fundamentally important concept for success in school, especially in college. Think of the best teacher that you have ever had. What made them a great teacher? I'm sure some of you are thinking about the teachers who gave out lots of candy or didn't enforce any rules, but I mean think of the teachers where you actually learned a lot. What was it about this teacher? Was it what they said? How they acted? Or what they did to help you learn? Most people remember a class that was interactive, that had assignments and activities that were interesting and provided multiple ways of learning. The teacher helped to inspire and engage you in the material and increased your motivation to learn. They were probably funny and passionate about what they were teaching.

Now think of the worst teacher you have ever had. Mr. Dufus, football coach and geometry teacher who went into teaching because his small business failed and he wanted his summers off. He looked forward to the end of the day when he could get back to coaching the football team and hazing the nerds who walked by the locker room. He probably handed out worksheets and boring textbooks. At 8am, he melted into his chair and then pointed to the chalkboard with a long stick so he didn't have to get up until lunch. On Fridays he showed civil war movies on VHS while he came up with his offensive game plan for the big game that weekend and didn't notice or care that you were sleeping. He used the same tests he'd been using since 1973, and had someone else grade them for him, if he bothered grading them at all.

What is the difference between these two classes? One class inspired you to learn and the other class sucked every ounce of your motivation to learn. But the one thing that was constant was your ability to learn. Both classes offered materials and information that was available for you to learn. Mr. Dufus probably had a text book with interesting information in it, if he had actually read it. His ability to teach you this material was pathetic, but your ability to learn the information didn't change. It was still the same *you* in the course with Teacher of the Year and your ability to learn wasn't any different. The difference between the two courses was the teaching, not your ability to learn.

Teaching is only one aspect of learning. Learning is a choice. The best teacher in the world could stand on tables, make objects levitate, and do backflips, but if you weren't interested in learning the material you could make a choice not to learn. Some teachers offer more resources to aid and inspire your learning, but if you don't access the resources or engage with them, they are as useless as Mr. Dufus. The responsibility for learning is on you and you alone.

People often think that learning requires sitting and listening while a teacher fills up your brain with information. But in reality, the process of learning is so much more interactive. Some teachers provide this interaction for you and motivate you to engage, and other teachers set the material in front of you and expect you to teach the material to yourself, otherwise known as learning.

Why is this so important? Because at the end of the day, you dictate your learning and you have the power to control it, regardless of who is in front of you or how they are trying to teach you. As we discussed, professors aren't teachers by trade, they have limited instruction in how to be good teachers and in many colleges, are barely held accountable for their ability to teach.

More importantly, professors are not necessarily experts on how their students learn. You are the expert in how you learn and you have to master this skill. No one will and no one can make you learn. That is your choice. This is not to say that the teacher's ability is irrelevant; bad teachers are a damn shame and great teachers inspire you to learn. But at the end of the day, the learning part is your responsibility.

College classrooms are very different from high school. College professors are likely only willing to do so much to help you learn the material. Think of a college professor as a waiter. You ordered a plethora of delicious food and their job is to bring it to your table. Some professors will tell you how it was made and describe how delicious it is and maybe how to eat it. They might even spoon feed a little into your mouth and wipe your dribble as you nibble it. Other waiters — and professors — are just going to toss it on the table and go take a smoke break diner style. It's your choice to eat it, your choice to appreciate it, your choice to chew it, and your choice to wipe your bottom lip. The food didn't change, the delivery did.

You can change professors, take a required course at a different time or even at a different college, you can read all the reviews and talk to upperclassmen, but even with all of your proactive efforts eventually everyone is stuck with a bad professor. But remember, for every class with a terrible professor, there will be a certain number of people in that class who get A's. They didn't benefit from the shoddy teaching any more than the students with F's. It sucked for everyone. What they did, though, was focus on their ability to learn the material in spite of the terrible teaching. This will be your responsibility in every class, regardless of who's teaching it.

So, understanding what you will need to learn in each course is essential. Consider all of your resources, all of your learning preferences, all of your strengths and weaknesses and take responsibility for your learning. Whether it's finding someone to tutor you outside of class, someone to study with, spending more time reading the material and taking notes, or watching someone else teach the material on YouTube. You'll need to do whatever you can to assure your learning.

The Classroom Environment

College classrooms can vary from huge lecture halls to small classrooms. Some classrooms will have tables and others will have desks. Some classrooms will be held around a table in a conference room and others will be held in science labs. Some will even be re-purposed storage rooms or infirmaries. However, there are some similarities between all college classes.

First, every student who is sitting in the classroom recognizes that they chose to walk through the door. Thus, students are generally more serious. Additionally, most college classrooms will have a wide array of learners, from true freshman to 30-something military veterans to people your parents' age returning to college. Each classroom will also have students who act like someone forced them to be there and a group of students who are excited to learn.

What you need to remember is that college is not high school. You have made a choice to walk through that door and thus you have the responsibility to take it seriously. If you wear your pajamas, sit in the back, and try to hide your eyes as you nap, no one will take you seriously. Especially not the professor. Think of the college classroom as arriving for the most important job you have each day. Act professionally, be mature, and play the part. Sit where you know the location will provide you with the best opportunity to learn. Dress in clothes that reflect your interest in learning and your professionalism. Come on time and prepared for class.

If you look and act like a high schooler, people will treat you like one. Act like a college student who is there to learn.

The Sacred Syllabi

Behold the syllabus, like the words of the Academic Gods handed down to you upon sacred tablets of goldenrod 8.5x11 paper. The syllabus smells of fresh copy machine chemicals and contains the commandments of the mighty professor which provides you the key to unlock their divine knowledge. Or, maybe it imparts further confusion and mystery.

Your syllabi (the fancy way of saying syllabuses) will be roadmaps to everything you need to know in your courses, from course readings to assignment due dates to exam times, and even fascinating confidentiality statements and conduct disclosures. Professors often climb mountains or sit under large trees for enlightenment to create their syllabi, or at least they act like they do. Since the beginning of time, a professor's favorite response to a course question is "it's in the syllabus." You will undoubtedly hear it in each class and hopefully you weren't the one who had dishonored them by asking such an ignorant question. The syllabus is so important that the first day of class is "syllabus day." You get an entire class meeting to listen to the professor proclaim the words of the syllabus, and then let you go early. Presumably, that's so you have extra time to spend beholding the splendor of their sacred text. But seriously — be sure to read the syllabus. Know the syllabus. Be the syllabus. The syllabus is your friend or your enemy, but it matters a lot more than you think.

On syllabus day, along with the holy writ, most professors will also provide you with their expectations. At this introductory setting, they may tell you to raise your hand before speaking or just allow you to comment and ask questions freely. They may give you their expectations for participation and how to participate appropriately. They may have a policy about using technology in class, such as laptops or recorders. Assume that most professors don't want you to ask permission to use the restroom, you can just quietly leave and do your business.

What to Expect

It's important to understand the expectations within each class and the way you would like to be received by your professor and fellow students. It is expected that you participate in class, by not only listening and taking notes, but also offering your questions and answers during discussion. You'll want to strike the right balance between talking too much and not talking enough. Answer the questions and participate when you have something worthwhile to contribute. Ask your professor to provide more detail or to clarify if she mentions something that sounded important to you but you failed to catch it. And then follow-up with more questions during office hours, if her answer doesn't clarify for you.

Here are some additional "Common Sense" guidelines that may not appear to be so common among freshmen:

- Turn off your cellphone. Don't just put it on vibrate, turn it off. There is nothing quite as frustrating to a professor as someone who is trying to secretly use their phone or if the class is interrupted by your phone call or text. No matter how subtle you think you are — you aren't. It can wait.

- Don't come to class late. But if you have to do so, quietly enter and be seated immediately. After the class, either send an email or stay after to apologize for being late. Don't make it a habit.

- Don't do other activities during class, such as crossword puzzles, Sudoku, other homework, or basket weaving (unless it's a class on basket weaving, of course). Like using a smartphone, this disregard will earn you similar disrespect from the professor.

- Don't talk to other people during lecture, even if you are whispering.

- Come prepared. At the very least, this means bringing a notepad, writing utensil, and the relevant textbook.

- If you want to eat during class, be sure to ask the professor before class to see if they are okay with it. Make sure it's a snack and not a full spread of sushi or a whole chicken. Don't be the jerk with the noisy wrapping paper.

- Raise your hand if you have a question or want to make a comment. If the professor nods at you or acknowledges that they see your hand up, you can take it down, they'll call on you when they are ready.
- Don't start packing up your things until the professor dismisses the class, even if they are talking when class is technically supposed to be over.
- There are no bells in college to tell you when to be in class. Be mindful of the time and be at least five minutes early and ready to learn.

"Back in the day", traditional college classes consisted of long, uninterrupted lectures. Students were expected to sit and listen and take notes while the professor held forth writing on the chalkboard. You will still find many courses still taught this way. However, professors have begun to rely on lecture as only one part of the course and now try to incorporate more discussions, small group discussions, and activities to enhance the course. During the lecture portion of the class, be sure to do your best with taking notes, but remember this is only one way to get the information. So, if you don't get everything they said, write down topics that you need to follow up on after class, either talking with your instructors during office hours or re-reading the subject matter in the textbook.

Don't consistently ask the professor to slow down or repeat what they just said. If you need to, adjust your note taking to keep up and try to paraphrase or get the main points. Often, you can request a copy of the PowerPoint notes, if they haven't given you them already. Professors often post their PowerPoint presentations before class, so be sure to print them if they are available. And, of course, if you have received a very helpful note taking accommodation, you can get a copy of the notes after class. Nevertheless, you should still try and take some notes on your own or at least pay close attention, during the lecture.

Professors often assign readings due prior to each class. Even though they will generally be covering the assigned reading, they expect that you have some familiarity with today's material so read the necessary readings before class. This is especially important during the discussion or group work component of the class. If you haven't read the material, you will have nothing worthwhile to contribute and it will show.

Do your best to contribute to the discussions. Answer questions that you know the answer to and offer your opinions when they are solicited. Don't dominate the discussions. If you realize that you are talking much more than anyone else, adjust the amount you are contributing to align with others in the class. If you realize that you are not contributing to discussions as much as anyone else, try to answer at least one question per class at the very least. If you have a lot of anxiety about talking in class, ask the professor if you could possibly have the discussion questions before class so that you could take some notes on them and be ready to share. This will help you become more comfortable with sharing over time.

During group work and activities, be a positive member of the group. This means sharing your ideas or thoughts respectfully. Don't dominate the discussion and don't just be a fly on the wall. Listen to other people's opinions in the group with an open mind and try to find common ground or see it from their perspective. It's okay if you disagree with people in your group, you may have to go along with the consensus though. When it's time for your group to share with the class, you can always discuss where you had disagreements, this will show that you were using your critical thinking skills and your ability to compromise. You can also always ask the professor to hear both sides and get their opinion. That doesn't mean that they are judge and jury. It just means they might help to clarify where your group is in disagreement. The professor is not only interested in the outcomes of the group work, but also to see how well you can work in the group. If you are always the person who is either doing nothing or starting fights in your group, it will reflect poorly on you, not your group.

Course Management Systems
Most colleges have adopted some content management system (CMS) software, such as Blackboard, Moodle, Canvas or Desire 2 Learn. Although

some professors rarely rely on these systems, others fully integrate it into their class. So… what is a CMS, and how is it different from a syllabus?

Along with Silicon Valley, online banking and Hollywood, academia also has leveraged "the cloud" to provide instant access to volumes of information. Your professor may use Blackboard or another CMS to post the syllabus, list assignments and readings, post grades, and provide handouts. Some professors may even use the discussion boards and other features to add programming flash and interactivity to assignments. Some coursework can mandate online discussion from the day's class. The CMS allows colleges to better evaluate student comprehension (and track participation) throughout the course, rather than only relying on formal testing. So, if they have put everything you need to know on Blackboard, you should know its content and rely on it. Again, like the deference around the syllabus as the final arbiter of course expectations, a professor who has taken the time to enter hours of information onto Blackboard will be quite aggrieved at a student who asks a question they should easily uncover, such as, "what do we have to read for next class?" or "when is the paper due?" Before asking, look on Blackboard to see if you can find the answer. Set your Blackboard to notify you of any changes before every class and make notes of important dates and deadlines.

Many colleges have gone "green" (otherwise known as "you pay for your own paper"). Thus, any readings or handouts will be available for you, printer-friendly, in your class account. If you want, print the materials and put them in a binder. Yes, you may be killing precious trees, but having a hard copy to reference in class and use to take notes will be worth the complaints from the forest.

Grading

Grading in college courses varies from professor to professor. Generally, your course grade will be "weighted" between various assignments, papers, projects, quizzes, and/or exams. The professor will usually provide a breakdown of the grading in the syllabus. Thus, you may have a class with ten small assignments totaling 25%, a midterm worth 25%, a paper worth

25%, and a final exam worth 25%. You'll probably even run into the dreaded course that has a midterm worth 50% of your grade and a final worth the other 50% of your grade. You should absolutely keep track of your grade and this all boils down to relatively simple math. Professors are always amused when someone comes to them after the course has ended and exclaims, "I don't know how I failed!"

Most professors also include the dreaded and mystifying "participation points" or something similarly obscure. These are the points that you earn for being a good student, as judged by the professor. They may take into account absences, participation in class, ability to work in a group, or your pleasant smile. Regardless, this is why it's essential to do all of the things we previously discussed; be on time, come prepared, work harmoniously in your groups, participate in discussions, and avoid using your phone during class. Grin and bear it all, when necessary.

Most colleges adopt an associated letter system to summarize your score. So, when you add up all of the points you earned in the class and divide by the total possible, the result relates to a letter grade. For example, 93% and above is an A, 88-92% is an AB or A- or B+, and so on. Many colleges don't give credit for anything below a C, so you may see the grading scale stop there instead of listing the point value for a D+. Knowing how your grade is adding up during and throughout the course will be essential for knowing how you are doing in real time and making adjustments in effort or finding additional support.

There are two approaches to grades. One is that "C's get degrees." Most folks put it in the form of a question:

Question: What do you call the guy who finished last in his class at Medical School?

Answer: A Doctor.

There is also the reality that your final GPA will impact your ability to get into graduate school. Even if you're not sure that is a path you will ever take, setting yourself up with options down the road is to your benefit. If graduate school is in the cards, plan on making a 3.0 or better. But don't let perfect be the enemy of good. Learn how to triage and prioritize. Yes, you probably could make that 37-page paper even better, and add even more primary sources to your exhaustive research — but you have to balance this desire for academic perfection with the reality that you also have other classes, meals to eat, and laundry to complete. Balance is key, and completion is often more important than perfection.

Take-Aways:

- Teaching isn't learning.
- The responsibility for learning is on you and you only.
- Understand what you need to do to learn in each course, regardless of the professor.

CHAPTER 10:

Virtual Learning

"For every benefit there is an equal and daunting negative for virtual learning, and so put your dreams of pajamas, comfortable couches, and body odor aside and really contemplate the important elements that should influence your decision on whether virtual learning is right for you."

With online learning, also known as virtual learning, becoming a more common modality over the past decade, college students will certainly see increasing opportunities to take some, if not most, of their classes from their computer. This may be exciting and/or terrifying news, depending on your learning style, but for those of you who have yet to take a class online, you should be skeptical at the very least. Virtual learning is the proverbial song of the mermaid, you can be easily lulled into the beauty, promise, and simplicity, to find out that you are about to be drowned by a spiteful, virtual sea creature. Yes, you can take a class in pajamas (against my prior recommendations), yes you don't have to go anywhere, and no you don't have to put on deodorant (but please remember your roommates). However, for every benefit there is an equal and daunting negative for virtual learning, and so put your dreams of pajamas, comfortable couches, and body odor aside and really contemplate the important elements that should influence your decision on whether virtual learning is right for you.

On the surface, online classes appear to be easier, and if implemented improperly, may be easier, but also less robust. Nevertheless, most students cozying up to their Cheerios, thinking they are happy to be home, are about to be smacked with the reality that online learning is tough, really tough. But there's good news, you can make it easier with some planning and discipline.

In order to talk about strategies to conquer online learning, we have to first talk about why it's harder and/or why being in-person is usually easier.

- **We learn from each other.** In fact, Lev Vygotsky, the Russian version of John Dewey, based his entire seminal learning theory around that fact. Whether we learn in formal small group discussions or activities or we learn from the questions people ask in class, much of our knowledge in school comes from the intentional environment. Some of this can be replicated via online learning, but we all know the challenges of online relationships, some more than others.

- **We rely on teachers, teaching us.** American schools are traditionally centered on a teacher-facilitated lecture paradigm. You show up, someone tells you what you need to know, you do some follow up reading, and you've learned something. If you aren't paying attention, the instructor either calls you out or gives you dirty looks. They hold you accountable. With virtual learning, there's still an instructor, but the actual dynamics of that relationship will be significantly altered, for example, you can mute their lecture at will.

- **School is more than learning.** Like all things in the world, school has its roses and thorns. We are in part motivated to learn by the opportunities outside of learning. Whether it's socializing with friends, intramural sports, or anime club, these activities provide balance in our lives to help regulate and endure the less motivating activities of classes. Will you lose some motivation to show up virtually when you don't get to see that cute person who you will awkwardly make small talk with or find comfort in group suffering through the depths of boredom?
- **Humans crave predictability.** There's nothing more American than the 40-hour work week with rigid start and end times and predetermined breaks in between. Whether we crave an unyielding itinerary in our lives or have been brainwashed to need it, the fact is that being on your *own time* can be overwhelming. The fodder for procrastination is loose deadlines and flexible work habits. Having a week to get it all done for some people is like saying you have ten minutes before the deadline to get it done for others.
- **School has less distractions, believe it or not.** It's hard to imagine being in a classroom with 20+ other students and not being distracted by the smacking of gum from the girl next to you, or the cologne from the guy behind you, or a casual smile from your *interest* across from you. But for the most part, the focus in a classroom is on learning, and it's not quite as easy to take a break to play some video games or grab a can of Coke and some cheesy puffs. Plus, the temptation to do today's class on the beach, in the bathroom, or on your car ride home will always be enticing, but won't be the relatively conducive, less distracting environment of a somewhat distracting classroom.

Some shocking news, if you haven't figured it out, we go to school to learn because it's easier and more effective than trying to do it from home. Whether it was the correspondence classes of the 60's, the conference call classes of the 90's, or the online education of this century, schools and colleges are still in business because it's a better pedagogical format for most students. This is not to say that virtual learning won't be necessary at times, preferable at times, or advantageous, so here is what you need to consider to make it a successful experience:

- **Learn Together.** Find a group of people to take the class with. Taking a class with a group will not only make the class easier, but it will also make it more enjoyable. Whether you already know some people in the class, need to reach out to the class list, or ask the instructor, find a group who would be willing to work together. Meet weekly in a coffee shop or have a twice weekly Zoom conference, but by all means, don't go it alone. A few companions on this ride will certainly help.

- **Teachers teach, students learn.** We've become overly dependent on needing teachers to learn. I know it sounds counterintuitive, but as I've made clear, the responsibility for learning will ultimately fall on your shoulders. As you have learned or are about to be slapped with this reality, the responsibility to learn the virtual material will be more of your responsibility than ever before. You can mute, pause, fast forward, slow-mo, or Facebook through any lecture now and the lecture is only one small part of mastering the class. Utilize the additional resources offered in the class; if they don't exist or are not sufficient, relentlessly find the resources to learn the material online, from your peers, or other smart people quarantined around you. The responsibility for learning is all yours now.

- **Plan some fun.** Do not overestimate the dark power of boredom. Finding the right work/life balance will be essential for online learning. Now, to be clear, this is not to excuse procrastination. In fact, procrastination is often a product of boredom. It's about planning fulfilling activities to offset the monotony of learning and improve your stamina to endure through it productively. Plan daily activities that you enjoy to keep the fun in your life and commit yourself to school when it's learning time. We all need something to look forward to.

- **Make a schedule.** On the surface, I'm sure you are looking at the flexibility of online learning with eagerness. But in reality, the lack of schedule can cause more stress and chaos in your life than you would expect. It's easy to be distracted by other priorities that pop up regularly or conversely, to become overwhelmed by an ominous, omnipresent learning environment. Thus, create a daily schedule that includes what courses you will be focusing on, what fun activities you will do, when you will take breaks, and when you will do "homework" and stick to it. Trying to do all of these things at once will be overwhelming and exhausting.

- **Limit your distractions.** True, I may have checked Facebook and my email a few times while writing this chapter, but also true, I'm not in school. If I were in school like you and actually needed to focus, I'd be in trouble. Whether it's Facebook, a Netflix series, snack breaks, video games, your iPhone, or staring at traffic, being home and learning comes with significantly more distractions than school. Make some rules for yourself, such as, no social media until you've done an hour of work or an hour of video games for every four hours of work. Use your devices' "Do Not Disturb" setting to protect your attention. Choose a workspace that limits distractions and just pretend like your teacher is watching. You know yourself the best, so set the rules and rewards/punishments to keep you focused.

At the end of the day, virtual learning is the classic six of one and half a dozen of the other and will shake out to be equally challenging as in-person learning, just in a different way. So, don't make the decision to take an online course, simply because you think it will be easier. This may be a valid factor in your decision once you've considered all of the above variables, but it's more about balancing your learning preferences, work/ life balance, and course content to make a fully informed decision. Plus, the more online courses you attend, you'll be missing out on some of the most essential reasons for *going* to college.

Take-Aways

- There is a reason why, regardless of the format, schools provide most of their learning in-person. These benefits certainly outweigh the value of virtual learning overall, so approach the decision to take classes online cautiously.
- Be sure to replicate the in-person learning environment as much as possible through group interactions, careful planning, and striking the right work/life balance.

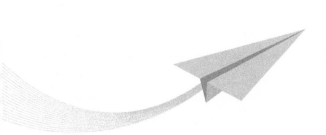

CHAPTER 11:

Knowing Your Resources

"As you now know, college has a lot of moving parts and someone to help you see the forest through the trees will be extremely helpful."

If you have ever had the misfortune of spending time in a hospital you know that as you laid in bed nursing your broken leg or missing your appendix all of the help you needed came to you. Your primary doctor would stop by, poke you a bit, and then order more services. Shortly thereafter, a specialist would stop by and poke you some more and possibly order some more services. Yet another specialist would show up and continue to prod you and poke you.

Imagine instead that if after breaking your leg, the ER doctor examined you and they told you that you probably needed an x-ray, so you should limp across town to the radiologist. After you crawled across town and had your leg x-rayed, all they said was, "yup, it's broken." Then they left the room. You probably would conclude from your television watching experience that you needed a cast. So, you again hobble across town to Springfield Cast and Crutch, where you get both. Then the assistant says "good luck" and leaves the room. As you can imagine, you probably need some more help, but have no idea where to go next.

This is a very good analogy for the difference between high school and college. In high school, teachers and administrators were responsible for tracking your progress and intervening when you needed help. If you needed help writing papers, they would assign you a writing tutor. If you were failing in math, they required that you attend an additional math study hall for help. If you were feeling extra sad, a teacher might send you to a guidance counselor. And if you were failing exams, they would give you an accommodation for extra time on tests. All of the services were under one roof and the staff assisted you in accessing them. They would bring them to you — maybe before you even realized you needed help.

In college, it's almost the opposite. You may have an adviser who reviews your performance every semester making recommendations, but it's unlikely they'll do much more than that. If you are failing in a class, a professor may recommend you get additional help. But that's if they notice or care that you are failing. They won't set it up for you. In college, accessing these supports and services will ultimately be up to you. Diagnosing what you need and where to find it will ultimately be your responsibility. Most colleges have a plethora of supports and services, but no one is going to walk you through the door. Therefore, you will need to know what is available, where it is, how to access it and when you need it.

Advising

Depending on the college, your adviser will either be a professor who has been assigned to you or someone in the college's advising office. They are there to help you strategize about which classes to take and when. They help you decide what your major will be and support with other bureaucratic processes. You will likely meet with your adviser once a semester and you will likely have to wait in a line to see them. Most advisers on college campuses are overloaded with an unreasonable caseload and don't have the time to do much beyond their stated expectations. Some highly dedicated advisers may help you problem solve issues in class or give sage advice on your performance. They are rare. But most good advisers will listen to your concerns or problems and then recommend more qualified people to talk with. Average advisers will allot you the necessary 30 minutes each semester that it will take to determine classes for the following semester, then send you on your way.

You should establish a positive relationship with your adviser and make it a point to see them more than once a semester. It will be to your advantage to have a relationship with them and keep them up to speed on your progress. At the very least, schedule an appointment with them at the beginning, middle and end of each semester. If you are struggling in a class, see them sooner and be frank about your struggles. Let them know what you are doing to deal with the trouble, and ask for their recommendations. A good adviser may have great suggestions but will definitely have great connections; an informed adviser is a precious advocate.

Conversely, be sure to consider the menu of options on campus to assist in your education if you end up with an adviser who isn't being helpful or available. Ask the secretary in the advising office about switching to a different adviser. Don't worry, you won't offend your adviser. Remember, they have a huge caseload and one less person is a win, as far as they are concerned.

Most colleges that assign professors to be advisers also have an advising office. In fact, your professor likely has the advising office on speed dial for those special cases where they run into a problem that will take up too much of their time, or possibly, they admit they don't know the answer. If every professor was good at being an adviser, an advising office would be obsolete. So, keep in mind that there a some "real" advisers who may be able to help more effectively.

If you feel like your issues exceed the pay scale of your professor, there is nothing stopping you from requesting a meeting with someone in the advising office directly. In fact, the advising office also has some power that your professor may not have. For example, if you are on the waitlist for a class that you really need, the advising office can call the professor offering that course and see if they'll make an exception. Sometimes a professor is more willing to work with the Advising Office than with an individual student. And, if not, the Advising Office may be able to override the registration system and enroll you in classes in certain situations.

Another huge advantage that a professional adviser may wield is they may be more adept at identifying any issues you are having and make more qualified recommendations for solving these problems. The advising office will often work closely with all of the other student service offices, so they may be more aware of strategies and support than your faculty adviser was aware of. If your adviser succeeded in any way that you were unable, be very grateful, and also make a follow-up appointment; this person is a great resource you must cultivate.

Disability Office

If you have a documented disability you will be assigned a disability counselor in the disability services office. This person will ensure that the college is meeting their ADA requirements and will help you determine your accommodations, ensure you receive your accommodations, and hopefully advocate for your rights when necessary. Unfortunately, as we previously discussed, as colleges have begun to shrink their budgets while simultaneously more students with disabilities have begun to attend college, caseloads have increased dramatically for disability service offices. Thus, you may be in another situation where you are one of hundreds of people on your disability counselor's caseload. As is the college rule, they do not feel obligated to seek you out, you will have to go to them. In many cases, in fact, you will have to advocate for them to advocate for you.

The disability service office is extremely powerful on campus. For one, colleges do not like getting sued. So, they will generally defer to the opinion of the disability service office if an issue arises. Secondly, professors will generally take the advice of the disability service office and therefore they can pull strings for you when necessary. In other words, do not dismiss this resource, out of some misplaced sense of pride. You may need them at some point and establishing a positive relationship with your disability service counselor, the director of disability services, and most importantly, the secretary will be crucial.

If you have some timidness or shame in using the disability service office you are not alone. But remember, colleges weren't created for your diverse learning needs and this office attempts to level the playing field to increase your opportunities for success. Now don't expect your disability counselor to be your burly bodyguard shadowing your every move, threatening to break the legs of anyone who violates your rights. Rather, it will be on you to stay in frequent contact with your disability service counselor. At the very minimum, meet with them every semester before classes start to review your courses and accommodations. Better yet, stop by the office every week to say hello. Not only will you be more comfortable working with them when you need them, you will likely also meet a lot of other awesome students who are on a similar path. In fact, many disability service offices offer group study sessions, student events, and other opportunities for you to collaborate with others.

Smart Students Leverage the Writing Center

Here's the truth: EVERYONE needs help with writing. Every professor you will encounter asks someone else to edit their papers. Some professors even hire professional editors to edit their work. In fact, some professors are terrible writers, even the ones who will be grading your writing and judging that you are a terrible writer. Not to mention that after your professors have someone edit their papers, they then submit them to a review board which edits those same papers again. In fact, it's not uncommon that the review board tells them to revise their paper and resubmit it. If you think that you can write a paper on your own, edit it on your own, and submit it on your own with the best results, you are in a class of your own.

Whereas high school probably had a lot of quizzes, tests, projects, and dioramas for the diorama-rama, college requires much more writing. Writing assignments in college will be your most daunting task, even if you are great writer. They are time consuming, come with high expectations, and are graded subjectively by professors. It is a requirement to be a proficient writer in college. The days of alternative assignments are over. However, being a proficient writer does not require the ability to write perfectly the first time. A proficient writer is someone who is able to create an engaging and purposeful product and this will take more effort than just screen time. Fortunately, almost every college has a writing center to help you.

The writing center is generally staffed by students and staff who have been trained to assist you in writing papers and are there to help you with the entire writing process. Often writing centers suggest you come to them at the first stage of the writing process, the planning stage. They can help you organize your thoughts into a cogent paper and help you plan out the structure. They can then work with you throughout the process. However, even if you have written the paper and have either run into some issues or just need someone to review it, they will generally help at any stage in the process. What most writing centers will not do is to read your paper and use a red pen to correct your mistakes before handing it back to you. They are more interested in teaching you the best strategies and methods for writing a good paper and making general recommendations to improve your writing. They will also likely have a sign somewhere in the office that says, "A lack of planning on your part does not constitute an emergency on my part." So, they are not there to help you speed write or revise a paper the night before it is due.

You must use the writing center. Writing centers are not there for bad writers. Writing centers are there for people who want to be excellent writers. Thus, you will see honor students, athletes, diverse learners, and even graduate students in the writing center. Everyone needs help with writing. So which papers should you use the writing center for? All of them. Or at very least, every major paper, i.e., papers that will have a large impact on your grade in a class. However, even if you are getting negative feedback in a class where there are multiple small papers due, go to the writing center for assistance. If you try to write a major paper in a class and bomb on it, there is nothing the writing center can do for you.

So, make it a practice of starting every paper with the writing center and over time you can decide to what extent you will need their continued support. Additionally, attend their writing workshops and seminars. Improving your writing throughout college will only make your life easier and less stressful. Go to the writing center.

Math Lab

As you probably suspect, most people who take Math classes at the college level, or even the high school level, eventually forget most of what they were taught. Remember the days of trying to figure out who actually uses proofs in Geometry or the rationale for linear equations, inequalities, graphs, matrices, polynomials and radical expressions? As you suspected, for most people math classes were a hurdle that they just jumped over as gracefully and with as little damage as possible. Most college students will have to take at least one math class. For those of you pursuing a math related degree, well you know what you just signed up for. The difficulty with taking math classes in college is that they exceed the knowledge and skills of most people around you. So, asking your buddy to help explain the difference between a sine and cosine will probably be fruitless.

Additionally, most math classes are taught by math people. Without generalizing too much, people who have chosen to spend their lives with numbers may struggle to convey complexities in an engaging fashion. Not to worry, most colleges have a Math Center or Math Lab similar to the writing center.

Math labs are usually staffed by people who like math and also want to help other people learn math. So, when you need help with nonlinear equations, these people will speak your language. If you know that you struggle with math and are taking a math course, start with the lab at the beginning of the semester. Often times, they will offer group study sessions where you can stop in and just do your homework around other people who struggle with math. This will allow you to ask questions in real time and improve your skills. As with most subjects, math is often taught progressively, so you need to have developed the skills from the previous class to be successful in the next. Thus, falling behind in your math class is like running the same speed on a treadmill that keeps speeding up — eventually you're going to end up on your face. You need to stay on top of it as the course progresses, and the math lab can help you keep up the pace.

Coaches and Tutors

Most colleges have some office or staff member that helps students find coaches and tutors. Most likely the offices we just discussed will have a list of tutors that you can access, but there may also be other options. First you need to know the difference between coaching and tutoring.

Generally, tutors will help you learn and understand concepts specific to a content area. Accordingly, a math tutor will help you in Calculus and a science tutor will help you in Biology. They will help you learn the concepts and answer your questions; they have an expertise in a particular course area. They will probably not care whether you finish the assignment they helped you with nor help you plan your time wisely to study.

On the other hand, a coach will help you strategize how to best approach and manage a difficult class or schedule of classes. They may be able to help you with some content, however, they will probably refer you to a tutor as part of their coaching plan. They are more likely to help you plan out the best use of your time, help solve problems, encourage you to advocate for yourself when necessary, and help hold you accountable to your goals. Depending on your strengths or challenges, you may not need a coach.

For students with ADHD, anxiety, or depression, having someone there to help you stay on top of things may be the only thing you need while students who are very organized and motivated may just need tutors to help with difficult assignments, but can manage their course load effectively. You should be reflective and aware of what you might need. Certainly, a coach can be helpful to anyone and if you are unsure, starting with someone would be wise. As you now know, college has a lot of moving parts and someone to help you see the forest through the trees will be extremely helpful. Just be sure to be proactive and seek out coaching and/or tutoring before you start struggling. Planning for the struggle will always lead to a less stressful and more successful semester.

Now for the bad news. Although colleges probably have a list of free coaches and tutors, you will also be given a list of coaches and tutors that charge by the hour. These professional coaches and tutors make a living helping students become successful and have the expertise and desire to assist you. For those of you who are still calculating the cost of college, the idea of paying someone else may seem daunting. Nevertheless, the price of a semester in which you fail your classes is much less cost effective than hiring someone to help you rescue your first attempt.

If you do decide to hire a coach or a tutor, do some homework first. Find out who knows the people on the list and share with them what you are looking for and ask who might be a good fit. Contact this person and see if you can meet with them first to see if you like their Big Picture approach and techniques. Consider asking about their availability and their willingness to meet with you when you may need them more, where they are willing to meet you, how frequently they recommend meeting, and the process they will use to help you. You can also ask your potential coach/tutor for references - someone who they already work with. You will be paying this person, so it's in your best interest to be sure they are worth every penny.

If you are going to be paying someone to coach or tutor you, you may also want to explore the option of remote coaches and tutors. There has been a dramatic increase in online services that will provide people to will meet with you via Facetime or Skype. Given their ability to reach more students around the country, their prices may be more competitive and you may find that meeting over the computer may be just as effective as meeting someone in person. Organizations such as Tutor.com and Lifecoach.com can assist you in finding a person who can meet your needs and expand your options beyond just the local coaches/tutors, and possibly save you some travel time, scheduling constraints and money.

Counseling Center

The actress Jenny Mollen said, "There are two types of people in this world: those who think everyone needs therapy, and those who have never been." Counseling and therapy have been stigmatized in our society. It's common for people to think that therapy is only for crazy and/or depressed people. However, that could not be further from the truth.

Therapy is your opportunity to evaluate your best self and work around the obstacles to becoming that person. You do not need to have a "problem" to see a therapist. In fact, many people who see therapists have the least problems. There is no shame in seeing a counselor or therapist, in fact, there should be some pride in your willingness to be proactive in seeking someone to help you face your challenges. College is a time of awkward transition and overwhelming transformations, and finding someone to help you navigate through these times will be extremely beneficial, if not absolutely necessary.

Fortunately, most colleges have a Counseling Center where they offer free counseling and therapy. These are people who work with college students every day and know the struggles and challenges of college. They know what you will be going through and can help you sort out your life before it becomes overwhelming. You can stop by or even send the counseling center an email saying, "I'd like to see someone who can help me be more successful in college."

Your first meeting will probably be a little awkward. It might not be, but be prepared for awkward. Once you get to know the therapist, you will have an invaluable person in your corner. If you spend a few sessions with this person and don't find them valuable, you can always switch to a different therapist. Or, even decide it's not for you. Regardless, do yourself a favor and use the counseling center. You will be a better person for it.

Health and Wellness Center

Larger colleges and universities will usually have a student health and wellness center. For those of you who aren't "townies," you will not have the luxury of popping into your doctor when you are feeling a bit under the weather. Given this is the case for many college students, colleges provide a health center on campus to get you feeling well again. Health centers will usually take your insurance and also communicate with your primary doctor at home to provide you with the appropriate care. You will most likely no longer have your mother available to point out that you are oozing toxic yellow phlegm from your nose or to feel your forehead to say you have a fever. So be proactive and take advantage of the health center when you are not feeling right.

It's best to stop in as soon as you feel sick and get treated, rather than wait and spread your illness to all of those around you, while at the same time you are becoming so seriously ill that you end up missing weeks of important classes. Moreover, you'll likely hear about the horror stories of college student plagues. There will be rumors of the vicious kissing disease, Mono. There will be tales of staph infections from the gym, and even the very dangerous meningitis. It's best to rule those things out early, rather than letting them fester, sometimes literally.

You should also use the Health Center to get your annual flu shot. No, the flu shot doesn't give you the flu, rather it will protect you against the inevitable flu epidemic that will assuredly inflict your friends who think the flu shot doesn't work.

Take-Aways:

- There is no such thing as too much support, so leverage all of the services that are available.
- You need to identify how you might struggle and also when you are struggling and take the steps to seek the support before you fail.

CHAPTER 12:

Assistive Technology

"Whatever the original intent, calendars have come a long way since they were inscribed on large pieces of stone and now come in paper form with options like Cute Puppies, Unicorns, and Inspiring Messages with Mountains and Sunsets."

"*C*ome on, Frank!"
    "*I'm coming, I just need to find my (fill in the blank)!*"
This was how most exchanges began when leaving the house with my fun-loving, big-hearted, and total mess of a roommate, Frank. To say Frank had the attention span of a squirrel would be doing a disservice to squirrels everywhere. He was a hard worker and loved by everyone who knew him, but he was usually a flurry of missed appointments, late arrivals to work, missing keys and lost wallets.

Our fellow roommates thought it was funny for the most part, and we would do our best to be Frank's on-the-fly secretary. But when it impacted our life, we would get slightly frustrated. Like the time we couldn't find the television remote for a month, until we were all golfing and Frank found it in his golf bag. Or the time we could hear the phone ringing, but couldn't find it, only to realize that it was in the oven. Daily life with Frank was a thrill ride.

It was Spring Break of my Junior year and all of our roommates were planning a trip to New Orleans. We were taking a shuttle from our house to the airport and for days we were mostly focused on getting Frank there.

"Frank, did you pack your contacts? Frank, did you remember to ask off from work? Frank, did you find your suitcase yet?"

We all knew that getting there with Frank would be next to miraculous. As the shuttle pulled up, Frank was still stuffing things into his bag, one lost sock at a time. We were all waiting outside with a tight window to catch our flight. The shuttle was honking its horn, we were yelling out the window, and one roommate was at Frank's side acting like a swim coach cajoling him at the side of the pool as he finished his last lap. He was almost ready when I yelled up, "Don't let Frank forget his driver's license!"

It was the death blow and our final straw. Frank couldn't find his wallet. After waiting for at least 30 minutes while he tore up our entire apartment looking for it, we left him behind, and in the process, we all missed our flight. We eventually got to New Orleans. Frank found his wallet already packed in his suitcase, but we were all beyond fed up.

When we all got back from New Orleans, we had an apartment meeting without Frank. Should we kick him out? No, way too good of a guy and way too much fun. Should we hire him a helper monkey? No pets allowed in the apartment. Should we have his Mom move in? Yes, but she had already said, "Good luck, he's yours now" to us as she moved him in a year ago. It was then that one of my roommates remembered reading about this new piece of technology that might do the trick. It was a key finder device, but it could be used for anything.

The device had a central unit with six colored buttons on it. It was the size of a tv remote control, and each button was connected with a small square tag. When you pushed the button, a tag would ring. It was the device from the gods and we all chipped in and bought it for Frank.

We made the effort to assign the tags to the six things Frank lost the most: his keys, wallet, laptop bag, remote control, phone, and glasses case. We tested each of them out to be sure they worked and we were on our way to Easy Street.

At first, we used the device the most. Frank would walk into the room and say, "Uh, has anyone seen my wallet?" and we would simply press the red button and follow the beeping to the inner depths of our apartment. Or when we were heading out for the night and we could see Frank conspicuously looking around the apartment, we would push the green button to beep the location of his phone. We would even do a "readiness check" where we would make Frank stand in the kitchen and press all six buttons to be sure he had everything he needed and that he wasn't bringing the remote control with him. Life was good with our new technology and Frank even began using it himself.

That was until we were loading up to go to an NBA basketball game and Frank was still in the house as we all were standing outside waiting for him. Of course, we had his ticket, but we left the other items up to him.

He yelled down from the window, "Have you guys seen my wallet?" And we yelled up, "Push the button!"

And then, "Have you guys seen my phone?" And we yelled, "Push the button!"

"Have you seen my glasses!" And we yelled, "Push the damn button, Frank!"

We waited about ten more minutes until we finally decided to go back upstairs to see why we had regressed into the old days of hide and go seek with Frank's essential items.

When we entered the apartment, Frank was in a frenzy pulling off cushions from the couch, looking under the radiator, and taking all of the clothes out of his closet. We couldn't understand why he wasn't just pushing the magic button to find his things. So, we went into the kitchen to do it for him. What we discovered was shocking — missing from its usual spot between the phone and the dead plant was the central unit needed to beep his items.

My roommate yelled out nervously, "Frank, where is the central beeper unit for your tags?" Frank stopped what he was doing, walked into kitchen, and looked at us, defeated, and said, "I don't know, that's what I'm looking for."

Believe it or not, we actually never found that central unit. Frank remembers having it at one point when he was trying to find his keys, but that's all he remembers. Fortunately, we had come to love that sweet piece of technology so much, that we all chipped in to buy him another one. This time we duct taped it to the counter, so that at the very least, Frank would always know where one thing he owned was.

Frank's roommates

You might want to sit down for this, but here's some shocking news: technology is not just for gaming, updating people with what you ate for dinner, or for organizing Frank's life. In fact, assistive technology exists beyond the Content Management Systems we discussed earlier.

Assistive technology is a term that describes any piece of equipment designed to help you in your daily functions. The assistive technology market was originally geared just for students with disabilities, but is now taking off for everyone. Most people don't even realize that they are using assistive technology, but as they dictate text messages into their phone, ask Alexa to play their favorite song, or use word prediction to write an email, they are actually utilizing assistive technology.

These tools are meant to mainstream the mundane processes in our daily life and can certainly do the same for your college studies. What's even better is that most of the technology you already own can be used as assistive technology, so you don't have to buy new expensive equipment.

Wonderfully, many colleges also stock assistive technology centers where you can borrow equipment and try technologies to see if they help you.

Organization and Memory: Work Less by Working Smarter

The most difficult part of college for most students is managing a really complex and changing schedule. Unless your mom moved to college with you (which would be weird — don't let her do that), you will have to manage planning, remembering and then achieving your own schedule. In other words, you'll be following through on your adult responsibilities. But here is a great secret, there is a ton of technology to make this look easy. Let's start with the most common and simplest and then get into the more advanced options.

A calendar. Seriously.

This rare device was invented by the Ancient Egyptians and was used to keep track and try to predict the behavior of Ra, the Sun God, and the annual flooding of the Nile, or something like that. Whatever the original intent, calendars have come a long way since they were inscribed on large pieces of stone and now come in paper form with options like Cute Puppies, Unicorns, and Inspiring Messages with Mountains and Sunsets. They even make calendars in small book form, called Daily Planners. I bet you are thinking, this isn't assistive technology. But in reality, time-management applications are probably the oldest form of technology. They have been making sure that folks didn't miss their jousting lessons, or that they got a good spot at the beheading in the town square.

Even with all of the snazzy options available for calendar technology on your phone, laptop, or smart watch, many people still prefer just to write it down on their physical calendar where they can see it. If this works for you and you won't ignore your calendar or lose your daily planner, then by all means, simplify! Go real world. The key is to make this calendar your bible and use it for everything. Don't rely on your memory, write it down. Look at it every day and bring it with you everywhere. This will be your key to mastering timeliness and deadlines.

If you are someone who doesn't know how to use a pen, then there are a ton of great options available on any and all of your devices. Google Calendar is probably the most common calendar software and it syncs with your Gmail account, but Outlook and Apple iCal do basically the same thing. Regardless, using a digital calendar will give you access to a ton of features that the paper calendar will not. First, you can share your calendar across your laptop, phone, and any other connected device. Thus, you will almost always have a way to get access to it. Changing an appointment on one device syncs your schedule across your IT presence.

Another beneficial feature of a digital calendar is that you can set reminders. There is absolutely no reason not to set a reminder for everything on your calendar. This mother-replacing tool will send you alarms, texts, or emails to remind you of your important events and deadlines. What's even better is that you can set the reminder for a time when you actually need it.

For example, a reminder that only lets you know that you have an exam in Physics in ten minutes does you no good if it's the first time you are hearing about it. So instead, you can set a reminder for two weeks earlier to remind yourself to actually study.

Or, if your attention drifts easily and you need a reminder to stop playing video games so that you can run to class, you can set a reminder 15 minutes before each class. That gives you time to grab a banana, put your pants on, and slap some water on your bed head before making a run for it.

To be most effective, you MUST set reminders on your calendar and be sure any device you own is connected to the calendar (and unmuted!). It will be impossible to manage your daily life without a calendar in college, so make this your new best friend and put everything in your calendar. Put a reminder in your electronic calendar right now to put reminders in your calendar.

As we discussed, most colleges now have Content Management Systems (CMS), such as Blackboard, Moodle, Canvas or Desire2Learn. The functionality of these systems has advanced beyond just accessing your class syllabus and uploading your assignments. In fact, these CMS programs can also help you to organize your course schedule, set reminders, manage your calendar, and even integrate with your personal calendar. Again, you will have to do the work on the front end to make them work for you, but they are great tools for keeping track of your courses, assignments, and deadlines. Most colleges offer workshops on using this technology or even have a staff member who can help. You should absolutely spend the time to master this technology.

However, if you are faced with a college or course that does not offer or effectively use this technology, there are many quality programs that will help you manage your course load. MyHomework is one of the most highly rated digital student planners and is free to use. MyHomework allows you to enter your course schedule, upload your syllabi, set reminders for assignments, and even track your grades in each class. Utilizing MyHomework will help you to keep track of the endless number of assignments and organize your complex schedule in a way that is geared to college students. You can download this app on your laptop and your phone so that you always have quick access to your schedule and list of deadlines.

If you are going to use a system like this, be sure that you don't split your calendars. For example, don't put some things in Google Calendar and others in MyHomework. You'll find that having duplicates or even worse, thinking you put it in one and realizing it's in neither, will add complexity to your life that increases your stress. Again, like all assistive technology, it will only be as good as the data, and the amount that you use it. Embed this program or a similar program into your daily life and use it for everything. Enter everything and anything so that you will be lost without it. Relying on your memory for half of your schedule and the software for the other half will only result in twice the frustration. This program will be your new memory, so rely on it.

Voice-controlled Smart Speakers are the wave of the future, for the next few years at least. Smart Speakers, like Amazon's Echo or Apple Homepod, provide you with a personal assistant without someone moving into your house. Smart Speakers can integrate with your calendars, to-do lists, shopping lists, and even provide real time help with your homework. Alexa and Siri, the sophisticated and slightly flirtatious voices of Echo and Homepod, take away the need to open a device to enter reminders or items on your calendar.

You can simply say, "Alexa, remind me to take a shower tomorrow morning" and voila, she will be your new hygiene coach. You can ask questions like "Siri, what is a synonym for fantastic," and she will list "comical, eccentric, erratic, extravagant, and extreme" or "Alexa, what is the square root of 47?" and she'll tell you 6.855654. And when you are done studying, you can say "Siri, play some party music" and you'll be dancing your way to success. Because they need to know basically everything about you, you will need to make Siri or Alexa your new best friend, but not to worry, a recent study found that people actually begin having feelings for their Smart Speaker. In fact, there have been reports of families bringing Alexa along on vacations not to provide music, but so she's not alone. Hopefully, this new friend will make your life easier, just don't take it too far and begin going on dates with it. Some things a person just has to do on their own.

Digital Writing Tools: A Virtual Secretary

As you have probably realized by now, writing is going to be (one of) your most daunting tasks in college. Most classes require you to use writing skills for at least one assignment, if not every assignment. Even though going to the writing center can be helpful for organizing and revising your papers, most of the writing is going to be done all by your lonesome. Good news? Like organizing your schedule, there is a lot of technology that can assist you in your writing endeavors, much of which you probably already have access to. Finding the right technology to help you write your papers will make the process much easier and will result in better outcomes.

To begin with, your computer has a ton of features that can assist you in the writing process. Whether you are using Google Docs or Microsoft Word to write your paper, they have built in features that can help. First off, most writing specialists would agree that using a computer for writing is inherently more motivating and easier to create a quality product, quickly. Handwriting, if you know what that is, makes it more difficult to edit and revise your papers and is physically more cumbersome; also, many college courses do not accept hand-written submissions because they're harder to test for plagiarism. If you don't know how to actually type, there are tons of training apps that you can download to help teach you. In the longer run, you will save hours of your precious time.

It's probably also wise to determine a strategy for limiting your distractions while using your computer, such as logging out of social media. If your computer doesn't provide a "Do Not Disturb" notification switch, you can download a program like Freedom, that allows you to limit distractions for a set period of time while you are working. There's also the Productivity Owl, which provides an animated owl on your screen that taunts you for being distracted and suggests limiting time-wasting websites and apps while you write and study.

Handing in a paper with spelling errors is almost unheard of at this point, and to do so suggests an ignorance, laziness, or obstinacy that is hard to overlook. Both Microsoft Word and Google Docs have a suite of features that are essential for writing a good paper. The first, best feature is spell check (Google Docs calls it "Spelling and Grammar"). Spell Check gives you real time feedback on any misspelled word and even offers to correct the spelling in real time — just enable "auto-correct." Otherwise, when you are finished with your paper, have Spell Check review your entire document to detect your typos.

Grammar check also does a fairly good job of identifying some key errors in your grammar, and even offers some suggestions on correcting the mistake. A passive voice can be identified to you by grammar check (sorry passive voice), or more appropriately, grammar check identifies when you try to use a passive voice. Grammar check can also identify sentence fragments, capitalization errors, and other syntactical issues ("then/than", "they're/there/their", "it's/its", "your/you're" errors).

A more advanced feature is word prediction. You've probably already used this technology when writing texts on your phone. Well, your word processing software will likely have the same feature if you enable it. Word prediction anticipates the next word or words you will likely type and allows you to select it without typing it. Not only will this increase the speed of your writing, but can also help you be more accurate so that you don't make simple grammatical or spelling errors. Some word processing software programs have this feature built in; if not, there are numerous extensions and add-ons, such as $5/month Co:Writer Universal to provide the same function.

If you hate typing and/or are a slow typer, there are a variety of "speech-to-text" options available. In fact, both Google Docs and Microsoft Word have this feature built in. This is really no different than pressing the microphone icon on your phone and writing a text by speaking into your phone. And unlike your parents, you don't need to sound like a computer when speaking. You can talk in a normal voice and it will turn your speech into text. There is a learning curve for utilizing this feature and it can be frustrating when it misunderstands you, but if it's less frustrating and faster for you than typing, then you should definitely use it to your advantage. The most important factor is taking the time to carefully read back through your dictation to make sure that you haven't made any spelling or grammatical errors or that the computer didn't improperly substitute something embarrassing when you tried to use the word "sit" or "duck." That's not a conversation you want to have with a professor later.

The opposite of speech-to-text is text-to-speech. This may not seem like the most logical tool for writing, but for auditory-learners it's easier to process information when they hear it back. Accordingly, you can enable text-to-speech on your computer or download an add-on or extension, such as SpeakIt! This will allow you to either hear each word as you type it or you can select any passage and have it read back to you. Sometimes hearing a passage out loud will help you identify awkwardly worded sentences, so that you can go back and edit it. Basically, if any of your sentences sound like a brand-new foreign exchange student, you know it needs work.

Finally, there are a variety of software tools to assist you in planning and organizing your papers before you write them. It is never a good idea to just start writing a paper without planning first. As mentioned, most writing centers will start with some guidance on organizing your paper to make writing it easier. You have probably been taught how and why to create an outline, but some people benefit from being able to visualize the paper.

Graphic organizers can help you visualize the organization of your paper to ensure that it is logical and can assist you in breaking it down into parts for writing one section at a time. Programs such as Inspiration or Popplet can help you organize your Big Ideas visually and then create aspects and threads of your paper; some are free to use. Basically, you start with the main idea for the paper and then branch out main topics and subtopics into an interconnected web. Once you've mapped out your entire paper, the software converts the graphic organizer into an easy-to-follow outline so that you can now expound upon your thoughts. You can print out your graphic organizer to help you stay focused, remain organized philosophically and develop the literary architecture for your paper. If you haven't tried using a graphic organizer before, it's worth giving it a try to see if it unfolds an otherwise dense and tangled process for you.

Read-Aloud Apps

There is no way around it, you'll fit a lifetime of reading into your college career. Professors are only one part of your learning equation. Organizing how to read all the course material on a reasonable schedule is absolutely essential. This is a tall task for anyone. Throw in some reading difficulties or disabilities, and it makes keeping up almost impossible. This is precisely why taking a smaller caseload, preparing deserved accommodations, being scrupulous about which classes and which teachers you are taking each semester is crucial, whenever possible.

The added problem with college level reading is the assigned reading is not necessarily easy or entertaining to read. In fact, much of the reading in college also requires an additional level of interpretation that you will have to do on your own. Tackling the challenges of reading in college will be extremely important and fortunately there is some assistive technology that can help here, too.

Before getting into the various technologies that can be helpful, it's important to first determine what kind of reader you are, to determine what, if anything, will help. Reading is really no different than speaking in many ways. At some point, a wise cavewoman pointed at a deer and grunted "foooood". That verbal utterance had no meaning until the sound was associated with the animal — it is evident that the word food has no meaning to someone who doesn't know the reference. When that same wise cavewoman realized that someone couldn't hear her, she grabbed a rock and scratched some lines into a rock and pointed at the deer, and said "fooood." Now both the visual representation and the verbalization conferred the same meaning, i.e., let's eat (that deer). Both of these processes involve decoding, or the process of abstracting either the word or the stone etching and creating meaning from it.

Some people have an easier time decoding the grunt, while other people have an easier time decoding the etching. What's important to remember is that both abstractions refer to the same object. As long as you are eating venison, it is more important that the meaning transferred than precisely how you got the information.

So, think about it for a second, is it easier to listen to someone give you directions or do you need to read the directions? Are you someone who needs to read the directions out loud or are you someone who needs to hear them first and then read them? Are you someone who needs to listen to the directions and take notes or read them and highlight the important points? Each of these different cognitive translations will help determine what types of assistive technology will help you. The correct fit for you will be effective because your brain's mechanism for abstraction is assisted visually, auditorily, kinesthetically or in some combination.

As we discussed before, text to speech technologies read written words and speak them back to you in a creepy computer voice or a creepy seductive British computer voice. It's always a little creepy. So, if you are someone who prefers to listen, rather than read, or listen while reading this could be the right technology for you. There are a lot of software programs that will basically read anything for you that is written.

For example, you can install Natural Reader onto your computer and it will read aloud anything you select on your computer screen. Thus, you could highlight pages of texts and listen to them read back to you, or you can read along. Seeing that most printed material is also available in digital format, any handout, article, or reading from class could be read out loud to you by simply selecting the text you want read. Even better, there are huge databases of books and e-books that have been recorded by real people that have already done the reading for you. Audible.com, for example, has tens of thousands of books that have been recorded. If you can't find the book you are looking for, you can check with the college's library to see if the publisher provides an audio version of your course reading.

Maybe there is no clickable link to listen to the PDF your professor posted in your syllabus. Not to worry. If you can't find your book on audio or if your professor is relying on ancient handouts that don't have a digitized-content file available because he typed them on his typewriter in 1977, there are devices that can help. There are impressive optical character recognition technologies that convert written text and read it back to you.

For example, some software will allow you to scan or even take a picture of written text which it then converts into a text form to read aloud. Some Smartpens can convert written text into audio, so that you don't even need to upload the entire document; you simply trace over the text like a highlighter and the Smartpen will read the words out loud. Although this is slightly cumbersome, it can quickly help you interpret shorter passages when reading it is just not making any sense. Nevertheless, if you want something read out loud to you and this will help you, there is a way to do it.

Recording Tools: Say It Again

The flipside of reading in college is listening in college. Let's remember, your professors have spent decades focusing on the one topic that interests them the most. At every dinner party they attend, they corner unsuspecting guests and wow them with facts about the mating habits of pileated woodpeckers until they either trap someone else's attention or their victim nods off to sleep. You are a mostly imprisoned weekly guest at this exciting dinner party and your professor will be sure to tell you everything she knows. The challenge will be threefold: hearing everything she says, contrasted with knowing what is important to remember, and documenting it for later review. Doing this note-taking skill on the fly for many people is practically impossible. For those lucky enough to be good note takers, they will jot down as much as they think is important while the professor is talking. For others, this will be patting your stomach and rubbing your head at the same time. Therefore, you may want to consider using some assistive technology if you are not a skilled stomach-patting head rubber.

If you have difficulty listening to your professor, and simultaneously organizing future review notes, an option you may not have considered is to record the lecture. Even though you should ask for permission first, most professors will gladly let you record their ramblings, though some may wisely insist "audio only," to prevent unauthorized YouTube cameos. You can easily upload these files onto your computer or play them directly from the recorder while taking notes in the comfort and convenience of … wherever, and whenever, pausing as necessary.

There are also several apps, such as VSAuP, which modulate playback pitch so that you can slow down the lecture without the professor sounding like a scary ghost in slow motion. At a decent tempo, you will be able to write notes at a speed that is humanly possible. You could also try several speech-to-text apps to transcribe the audio into text (see Digital Writing Tools, above). However, the accuracy of these programs is very low, so don't rely on this alone.

Smartpens can also be used to help with note-taking and listening to lectures. For those of you who are mostly comfortable with taking notes while listening in class, you can use a smart pen to write your notes while it records the lecture. You can then relisten to the lecture or parts of the lecture that are associated with the notes you took. For example, you could write "WTF" at the part of the lecture that made no sense to you, and then after the lecture highlight your note and relisten to that portion of the lecture to see if you understood it the second or third time. Many Smartpens will also convert your handwritten text into digital text and give you the ability to merge your notes with the digitized recording.

Finally, for those of you with hearing challenges or even attentional issues, you can request the use of FM transmitters. This is basically a wireless microphone that you ask the professor to wear that transmits their voice clearer and louder into an earpiece or headphones that you wear in class. A college classroom can be distracting, so blocking out extraneous noise may allow you to focus on what the professor is saying better. Many of these devices also allow you to record at the same time, so you can kill two birds with one stone.

Of Course, There Are Digital Apps to Help with Math Too

There are a variety of assistive technologies for mathematics, although these tools are unlikely to level the playing field if math isn't your thing. Nevertheless, these tools may make your life a little easier or possibly make math slightly more palatable. Math notation tools allow you to type special numbers and symbols into equation format, so that you can read them more easily. They will also help you to organize your equations, so that they are easier to see and solve.

Calculators are obviously standard assistive technology, but there are also "talking calculators" that repeat the numbers and operations as you press them to ensure you are not making any mistakes.

Finally, there are math manipulatives, which is a fancy word for small toys that may help you to visualize a problem. Think using a toy pizza for learning fractions. These manipulatives can be actual physical objects or digital images on a computer screen. For example, many students use manipulatives in chemistry class to learn about molecules and the geometry of how they bind to one another. Having a physical representation of the molecules and bonds can help visualize an otherwise very confusing topic.

Take-Aways:

- Get a calendar, in any form, and use it.
- Understand your strengths and challenges and find the corresponding technology to assist you.
- Use technology to level the playing field and increase your chances for success.

CHAPTER 13:

Advocating for Your Needs

"There are a set of hidden rules that hang just below the surface that provide exceptions to even the most rigid rules in college."

I love rules. I have always loved rules. I'm good at following rules. I like to learn about rules. I like to follow the rules that I learn about. I like to know what to expect and when to expect it. I don't like surprises and I don't like places without rules. I love trains because there are a lot of rules and you almost always know what to expect, and unless it's a tragedy, they don't get off track (that's a train joke). If you haven't guessed, I have this special super power known as Autism Spectrum Disorder. It allows me to see the world through a different lens, gives me the ability to like trains and pretty much only trains, and it makes me great at following the rules.

When you have Autism, unexpected things and chaotic situations are like being in front of a speaker at a concert of whatever kind of music you hate. It's overwhelming and can make it difficult to focus on anything else. That's why I like rules: I know what to expect and I know how to comply. Literally, if I were on fire in front of a no smoking sign, I'd be more worried about breaking the rule than burning to death. This can make life challenging, because if you haven't noticed, people are always breaking the rules. Not to mention, there are these invisible secret rules no one tells you about until after you break them. Don't say something smells bad after someone uses your bathroom, even when everyone knows that it smells bad. Don't ask another woman if she is pregnant, even if she looks pregnant. Don't tell the man you have a crush on that you have a crush on him, instead be nice to him and smile at him, but don't smile too much at him, and never smell his hair, even if it smells like coconuts, which I would contend that that implies he wants people to smell his hair... long story.

I thought college was going to be perfect after I carefully examined the student handbook and the faculty handbook. There were so many rules — it was great! It was like I had a manual for college life and success would simply depend on following the stated rules. The handbooks had specific dates, timeframes, policies, exceptions to policies, and policies for exceptions. They provided local laws, state laws and federal laws. The college provided its own set of moral and ethical principles and even recommended what to wear to class. I was sure I had found the perfect environment for my super powers. Boy, was I wrong.

One of the first classes I took in college was an American Literature course. I was carrying a full load that semester, so it was one of my five classes. It was overwhelming for sure, but I was good at school so I knew I could handle it. In my Literature course, the professor asked us to post a class reflection online after each class discussing what we had learned that day. The rule was that you had to post it by 5pm after the class to have it graded, and it counted for 20% of our total grade.

Immediately after my Literature course, I finished the day with a Biology class, which I despised but the college rules were that I had to take Biology, so I took Biology. I had exactly 15 minutes to get to my Biology class after my Literature class, so I barely had time to use the bathroom and grab a soda. The rule in the Biology class was that you couldn't be late, so I was never late. My Biology class went until 5:00pm and the rule was that we couldn't do outside work in class and we couldn't leave early. Thus and therefore, I would not be able to submit my reflection on time. It seemed unfair, but those were the rules.

At the end of the semester, we had to turn in a final paper. My paper was on Emily Dickinson, mostly because anyone with Autism knows she's in the club after reading ten lines of her work. Anyway, I had worked tirelessly on this paper. I had several drafts, revisions, and rewrites. I reviewed the rules of the assignment numerous times to be sure they were all followed. The final rule was that no late papers would be accepted under any circumstances. The printed paper was due in the professor's office no later than noon on Saturday, double-spaced, 1" margins, no less than 15 and no more than 20 pages, in Times, Arial, or Helvetica font. I didn't think this would be a problem seeing that I had finished it days earlier.

I woke up Saturday morning and set an alarm to bring the paper to my professor at 11am. That would be enough time to be distracted on the way. As I went to print the paper, I received an error message. It said that my computer was not communicating with the printer. I tried not to panic and followed the directions on the tiny printer screen to try and get my printer online. After 45 minutes of messing with the settings and several hard restarts of my computer and printer, I got it to print.

I grabbed the paper and ran out the door. As I made my way across campus and into the Literature building, I glanced down at my watch and saw that the time was 12:01pm. I missed the deadline. My paper was late. No exceptions. I was upset, but those were the rules, and they were meant for following. I turned around and went home.

On Monday morning, I received an email from my professor asking if I would stop into her office that day during office hours. I assumed she had to follow the college rule to notify me that I was going to fail the class. I was there right at the beginning of her office hours ready to accept my failure. She opened the door and asked me to come in and sit down. I asked her if it was okay that I was wearing sandals, seeing there was a sign on her door that read "No shoes, no shirt, no service." She told me it was just a joke; I didn't get it.

Anyway, after I sat down, she took off her glasses and asked, "What happened? You were doing so well in my class and I really enjoyed your perspective. Why didn't you turn in your reflections or your final paper? I have to fail you and I hate failing bright students. My secretary said she saw you come into the office, look at your watch and leave."

Fortunately, I had brought a copy of the paper in my backpack and I pulled it out along with the rules she gave us for the paper and I explained, "I really enjoyed your class and I also really enjoyed writing the paper, but due to a printer problem, I missed the deadline by a minute."

"You mean, you wrote your entire paper and didn't turn it in because you were a minute late?" She looked shocked (and kind of funny, but you should never tell someone they look funny even when they do).

"Yes, you clearly stated in bullet point six that you would not accept any late papers under any circumstances. The rule totally makes sense to me, so no hard feelings."

"You could have absolutely still have turned it in. It was barely late."

"I'm sorry is there a calculation for determining when something is barely late vs. late no exceptions?"

"I just put that there so everyone knows how serious I am about turning things in on time. I wasn't even in my office that day. I'm sure people turned them in on Sunday, and I would have had no

way of knowing. I just wanted them here by Monday morning. If I say by Monday morning, people turn them in throughout the day on Monday, which doesn't give me enough time to grade them. So, I just say Saturday at noon to be on the safe side."

I stared at her with probably the most confused and perplexed look. This was not a rule that I knew, read, or could even possibly comprehend. So, I asked, "Is there a special rule about when class reflections are due?"

"No, I just want them in some time before the next class. If you could have gotten them done by 5pm after class, it would have been ideal, but not necessary. Wait, did you not turn them in because you couldn't get the done by 5pm?"

She was starting to understand my world. The good news was that after our meeting, she told me about the exceptions to her written rules and allowed me to turn in my paper and make up the reflections that I had not completed. It was at this time that I learned that there were as many hidden rules in college as there were written rules, if not a whole lot more.

Fortunately, my Literature professor offered to be my academic adviser and she helped me to interpret the endless stream of hidden rules throughout the next four years. Without her, I really would have failed, not just her class, but I would have failed out of college.

Rachel *(28), Transportation and Logistics Coordinator*

You've Got to Take Charge

No one is going to give it you. That's the hard truth in college. In high school, you likely had your parents, advocates, friends, siblings, and/or friendly teachers all working on your behalf. If you got what you thought was an unfair grade on your paper, your parents may have negotiated with the teacher. If you were sick, your mom called to excuse you. If you were skipping out of class, your friends may have covered for you. And if you were being treated poorly by the principal, your teacher may have been in your corner. But in "higher education", for the most part, you've got you and you alone covering your backside. Not only will your professors not speak to your parents, unless you've signed a release, it's illegal for them to talk about you with your parents. You are officially, and scholastically, an adult, if you want anything in college, you are going to have to grab it yourself.

You won't get arrested at the shopping mall for skipping class and the secretary isn't going to call your folks if you don't show up. Professors may care about your education, but they aren't going to force it on you. Think of college as a restaurant that you eat at every Wednesday. Every week you order the special of the day and a chocolate milk. The waiter knows your name, enjoys serving you, and even does his best to make sure you are happy with your meal. However, if you don't show up one week, the waiter isn't going to call to see if you're okay or if you need help. Moreover, if your french fries are cold, they won't know they made a mistake until you tell them. And, even though your burger comes with your much despised fried onions, they won't take them off unless you ask them. Complaining after the meal only means you didn't get what you wanted, when you could have easily fixed the situation.

Like a restaurant where you are actually getting what you want, your experience at college will be dictated by your ability to advocate for your needs and desires. In fact, advocating for what you want in college isn't only essential, it is expected. The college and faculty will follow their practices and procedures strictly, until you ask them to make an exception. Your grades and classroom expectations will be the same for you as everyone else, until you ask for them to be changed. Your professors will give you the grade they thought you deserved on your paper, until you challenge them on their reasoning. And, your final grade is only final until you've asked for a better final grade. Although college institutions may seem like a static, uncompromising place, it is like everything else in life, flexible.

But yes, on the surface, colleges may not seem flexible whatsoever. The policies, procedures, and rules may even have disclaimers saying that they are not flexible. However, there are a set of hidden rules that hang just below the surface that provide exceptions to even the most rigid rules in college. These hidden rules provide the flexibility of the policies and procedures that you will likely need at one or many times throughout college. Many of these exceptions to the rules may have an official form that just needs to be signed, you may just need to ask if that form exists.

Other exceptions may only be granted if you know who to ask and if you ask in the right way. It may not seem fair to bend the rules, until you realize that everyone around you is aware of these hidden rules and uses them to their advantage. If you don't, then you will be the one at an unfair disadvantage. The truth of the matter is that there are very few dead ends to your challenges in college, you just need to stand up for yourself and be willing to step around roadblocks. No one else is going to remove them for you.

Meet with Your Professor

As we discussed earlier, meeting with your professors regularly is of the utmost importance. Most of the exceptions that you will want can be granted by your individual professors. Let's assume that you've been preparing for class, arriving on time, not wearing pajama pants, asking the professor well-considered questions and answering the same from the teacher. If you have shown them that you are invested in the class, they may be much more willing to hear your case. This is why it's essential to meet with your professors regularly to discuss your progress in each course, to explore areas where you can improve, and to review assignments for corrective feedback. Not only will this increase your chances of doing well in the course, but it will also be useful if you need something from them. If the first time you meet with your professor is the first time you advocate for an exception, your chances will be unnecessarily slim.

So, what can you ask for in your courses, even if the syllabus says differently? Almost anything. The syllabus provides a list of general rules and policies that the professor will follow and expects the class to subscribe to... unless you ask otherwise. This doesn't mean you will get everything you ask for, but you will certainly get nothing if you don't ask. Here are some of the most common exceptions that are worth asking for, when you need them:

May I have an extension?

Although most of your assignments will come with a firm deadline and a note about not accepting late papers, when you get into a bind you can ask for an extension. Now this doesn't mean showing up to class the day your paper is due and asking for an extension. That's not going to work. Rather anticipating that you won't finish an assignment on time and asking at least a day in advance might. Honesty will always be your best bet. If you aren't going to finish your paper on time because you stayed up too late playing video games, just say that and explain you learned your lesson and will make the change in the future. Coming up with some extravagant lie that involves grandmas dying and flat tires will be easily seen through.

Remember, you are not the only one accessing these hidden rules, so your professor gets these requests regularly and they have heard many lies. You'll probably hear the college myth about the four students who missed their final exam because they were partying on Spring Break and asked to take it a day later. Their excuse was that they got a flat tire on the way home from a service trip. The professor allowed them to have an extension and when they sat for the final exam in separate rooms, the only question was, "Which tire?"

They would have been better off just being honest and appealing to the professor's good nature. You will also probably only get one or maybe two extensions. So, use them wisely and don't use them at all if you don't need to.

Can I make up the class I need to miss?

Although each class has a certain number of "allowed" absences, missing class is never wise. However, there are certainly times that missing class will be necessary or advantageous. Most professors will not expect you to ask permission to miss class, nor will they likely ask the reason.

Nevertheless, it will always be courteous and wise to anticipate the class or classes you will miss and inform the professor. Ask if there is any way you can make it up. If you were too busy vomiting into the toilet with the flu to ask before missing, sending an email after will also be okay.

Generally, professors won't have any way for you to make up the class, but it will show respect if you care enough to ask. However, if you have a good reason why you need to miss or why you missed class and your absence does affect your grade, then advocating to make it up is worth a try. And if they provide an opportunity for you to make up the missed time, you better do it. Just don't make a habit of skipping class.

Can I redo this assignment?
There will be at least one assignment that you wish you could have back. Whether you misunderstood the assignment or didn't put forth the effort that was necessary, there'll be times when you could have done better. You may realize your mistake as you turn it in, or when you get it back with a bad grade. If you know you can do better and know how you can do better, it may be worth asking if you can redo it. Explain the reasons why it wasn't your best foot forward and ask if there is any chance, they'd be willing to give you another shot at it. If you are lucky and they agree, be sure to knock it out of the park the second time and turn it back in by their deadline. If they say no, but you feel like it's worth them knowing that you are capable and care about the class, it may be worth redoing anyway and turning it in with your biggest puppy dog eyes. They may still not regrade it, but if the end of the semester requires a "benefit of the doubt", they may treat you more favorably.

Can I talk with you about the grade you gave me?
No matter what grading scale calculation, fancy rubric, narrative, or point tally your professor claims is an objective way of grading your assignments, the truth is that almost every grade you get in college is subjective (unless it's math—that's pretty objective).

Professors interpret your papers and assignments through the lens that they understand. Granted, they may be the expert in their subject area, but that doesn't mean that they are the expert in the way you demonstrate your understanding of the subject. If you get an exam, paper, or assignment back and you lost points in an area that you believe you got correct, you have every right to ask why. Not only will this help you to understand the material better, but it will also help you to adjust to how the professor grades your assignments in the future and show them you care about your grade.

Be sure to first research what the "correct" answer was and if you still think you have a case, be able to explain how they may have misunderstood your response. Then, make an appointment with them or go to office hours and provide the rationale for your answer. Ask if they would be willing to give you some or all of the points back. This is a respectable response and, if unsuccessful, there is no harm in trying.

Can I do any extra credit assignments?

Some professors will provide opportunities for extra credit listed in their syllabus. Other professors will only consider extra credit if you ask. The general rule of thumb is to always do the extra credit if it is offered, even when you don't think you will need to do it. Once the semester has passed and you receive your grade, there will be no opportunity to go back and do it after the fact. You will never know when you will truly need it.

If you bomb a test or paper and you know that your grade will suffer, it's always worth asking if there is any way to do some extra work to make up the points. You may even be able to suggest projects or assignments you would be willing to do if they would give you extra credit.

Can I do an alternative assignment?

Most of the assignments you are given in college are expected to be completed the same way as everyone in your class, unless you have specific accommodations granted by the Disability Services Office that allow for adaptations to the assignment. Having said that, it may be worth asking for an alternative assignment if you know that you will be unable to successfully complete the given task, or if you know that there is another way you could more effectively show that you understand the information.

For example, if you are asked to give an oral presentation in front of class and you have stage fright, you may ask if you could video yourself doing it. If a professor asks you to make a pretty poster and you are terrible at designing posters, you may ask if you can do a PowerPoint presentation instead. It's unlikely they will allow you to do something that will appear to be easier, but may be open if it takes similar or additional effort while still demonstrating your comprehension of the topic. If you can come up with an idea, it's worth asking. Otherwise, if you know the assignment is going to be problematic, you can explain why you will be challenged to complete the assignment and ask if there is another way you could do it.

Taking an "Incomplete"

Colleges generally have a policy on taking an "Incomplete" in a course. Similar to a letter grade, an incomplete is assigned at the end of the semester and shows up on your report card, reflecting that you haven't received a grade yet. Incompletes are usually reserved for situations in which outstanding circumstances prevented you from finishing the course on time: this could include illnesses, family emergencies, injuries or mental health challenges. When professors and administrators grant an incomplete, they are also accepting unexpected or extra work responsibility for themselves, and consequently, they make it more difficult and cumbersome to get an incomplete. However, in the right situation, an incomplete may save you from failing a course and give you the time you need to finish the course properly.

In the world of incompletes, having a connection with the counseling center and/or the disability services office will be beneficial. Both of these departments can make recommendations for granting an incomplete and your professor or dean will usually comply. Situations that may warrant an incomplete may involve anxiety or depression that caused significant absences, your disability preventing you from completing a major assignment on time, or your attentional issues causing you to miss a course requirement. Regardless, if you can anticipate that you won't be able to successfully complete a course in the allotted time, talk to your Disability Service Adviser or your mental health counselor to see if they believe it would warrant an incomplete request. If they agree, get them to write you a letter stating why and include it with your request.

To officially request an incomplete, you initiate the request with your professor. Explain the reasons why you think you are entitled to an incomplete, including any supporting paperwork. If the professor agrees, they will provide the requisite paperwork and develop a plan for completing the course. If they disagree and you still believe you have a strong case, you can appeal to the Department Chair and/or Dean. For an appeal to overrule the professor, a supporting letter from Disability Service, the counseling center, health center, or your doctor will be extremely helpful. Be sure to submit a well-written letter explaining why you believe you should receive an incomplete and suggest a timeframe for completing the assignments. Besides the extra work for your professor, another reason colleges don't like allowing incompletes is because students often don't finish the work. This causes all sorts of headaches for the college, especially if your instructor is an adjunct. The first answer on "Can I take an Incomplete?" is always no. But if you make the case well, and if you complete the work on time this is an avenue for your success during a hard semester. Don't plan on being given more than one incomplete in college though, and if you don't finish it, you definitely won't ever get another one.

Withdrawals

The goal for starting any class in college is to finish it with a passing grade. However, there are times when things won't go according to plan and you will be faced with either failing a course or limping through a course that you either hate or realize you don't need to take and hope you don't fail. The worst thing you can do in those situations is to just stop attending, resulting in a certain failing grade. This is usually completely unnecessary. Colleges allow students allotted time to determine if a course is a good fit and back out if necessary, without a penalty. Withdrawing from a course is always an option and often a good option if the course requirements appear to be beyond your present capability. You need to be aware of your college's policy around withdrawing from a course. Usually colleges provide three options: 1) early withdrawal without a penalty, 2) late withdrawal with a penalty, and 3) medical withdrawal with a potential penalty. All three options ultimately get you out of the course without affecting your GPA, but you need to know when to use them and how to use them.

Most colleges allow students to withdraw without a penalty within thirty days of the beginning of the course. This will allow you to sign up for a course and give it a test drive before completely committing to it. If you realize that the workload will be too great for your schedule, the professor doesn't jive with your style, or after a month of trying it out you realize you will ultimately fail it, you can request to withdraw from the course. If you do it within the early withdrawal time period, it will be like you never signed up and will likely get you a full refund.

Some colleges require a minimum course load for living on campus or being considered a matriculated (full time) student so you'll want to be sure that you are eligible to withdraw without adding another course. If you've checked with your adviser and you can withdraw, then it will certainly be better than wasting time on a course you will despise and/or ultimately fail. Every course will have aspects about it that you don't like, only withdraw if it is absolutely necessary.

If you miss the early withdrawal deadline and are stuck in a course that is intolerable or you know you are going to fail, all is not lost. Colleges provide a date for late withdrawal, often around eight weeks into the course. Deciding at this later date has some penalties.

First, you will likely have to pay for some or the entire course depending on when you withdraw. If you are using financial aid, some loan programs will require you to pay that money back. If you are using your parents' money, they will just be pissed, but probably less than if they had paid for you failing the course.

Second, instead of getting a traditional letter grade in the course, there will be a W next to the name of the course on the transcript, showing that you withdrew. Now this isn't the biggest deal, especially if you only have one or two in college. Some graduate schools, or schools you hope to transfer to, will be skeptical of someone who withdrew from a large number of courses. If neither of these are in your long-term plans, then you have less to worry about. In every case, a W will certainly be better than an F.

Finally, when all else fails, you may be entitled to applying for a Medical Withdrawal. A medical withdrawal may allow you to withdraw from the class after the late withdrawal deadline. It might even allow you to avoid the W on your transcript, or having to pay for the course. Similar to requesting an incomplete, having the backing of your doctor, counselor, or disability service adviser will be essential.

Basically, a medical withdrawal can be used if your health status prohibits your ability to complete the course. For example, if you break your leg halfway through the semester and don't think an incomplete makes sense, you can request to withdraw from the course without penalty. Colleges may still ask you to pay for part of the course, but you can always appeal and sometimes they will credit you for the next time you take it. This will also usually allow you to avoid getting the W on your transcript.

If your anxiety, depression, or other aspects of your disability interfere with the progress in your course, you may also be eligible for a medical withdrawal. You will most likely need a letter from one of those key offices. If you are nearing the end of the semester and you realize that your anxiety or depression has caused you to miss classes and assignments or impacted your ability to do quality work, you may want to explore a medical withdrawal from the class. Again, just deciding to stop attending will certainly result in a failing grade and rarely can you go back and ask for an exception after the fact.

Take-Aways:

- You need to understand both the rules and hidden rules of college to be successful.
- You need to ask for and use every exception and advantage in each of your courses, like everyone else.
- There is no reason to fail if you can see it coming.

CHAPTER 14:

College Life

"You will also need to be honest and self-aware about how ready you are to leave the nest because it's a long way to fall."

"*D*id you bring your toothbrush?"
"*Yes, Mom.*"
"*Did you remember your rain jacket?*"
"*Yes, Mom.*"
"*Did you pack extra underwear?*"
"*Yes, Mom. Please just don't worry about it. I will manage and you guys only live like two hours away. And there is the mail, and they do have stores in this town. What are you doing now?*"
"*I'm making your bed, it's probably the only time it will be made, so I'd like to be the one to do it. I brought your Star Wars sheets and your blankie.*"

"Mom! Put my blankie away! I mean, put that old dirty blanket away. Gently. In the top drawer. Can we just say goodbye now?"

That's when I realized what I truly meant to my mother. I was her everything but I was leaving and her house would finally be empty. As much as I thought she was looking forward to the day that my room became her sewing room and have some extra peace and quiet, it was only on this day that I fully understood how difficult college was going to be for her.

I drove her crazy on a regular basis, constantly argued with her, broke endless numbers of rules, and always complained when I was asked to help around the house. I didn't think anyone could possibly miss that, but through the slow stream of tears on her face, I knew leaving for college might be harder for her than it was for me. Everything I knew and found comfort in would only be small parts of an occasional visit. And as I experienced both my sister's and brother's transition to college, I knew that my home would be where I made it from now on. Sure, there would still be family dinners, vacations, and swims in the lake. But it was at this moment I realized that my childhood was over.

As my throat began to swell and my eyes began to fill, I hugged my mom and was able to say, "I love you. Thanks." But this was more than just a "thanks for making my bed, or moving me in, or embarrassing me with my blankie." This was a thanks for giving me everything I needed to have the confidence to do this. For making me cook dinner once a week to get ready for college. For insisting I do my own laundry. For making me stand up tall when I walked. For not only believing in me, but making me believe in myself. These were the gifts that she gave me that I would always have. And it was finally my time to use them.

"Where's Dad?"

"I don't know, he was talking to some kids down the hall telling them that they would have to meet you and joking about politics with them. He doesn't like stuff like this."

"What, going to college doesn't put hair on your chest?"

My dad was traditional in many ways. He was always claiming that certain things would put hair on my chest. I never wanted hair on my chest, but apparently this was a sign of something manly, so I figured if it grew, I did something right.

Drinking black coffee—hair on the chest.

Hot sauce—hair on the chest.

Shaving your face—hair on your chest.

Not getting stitches when you probably should have—hair on the chest.

Working up a sweat—hair on the chest.

Had this list of hairy chest recipes been accurate I would have been a gorilla at this point in my life. But I understood his point. It wasn't that he wanted me to be a "man," he wanted me to independent. He always said that if I do better in life than he did, it would be proof that he did his job. His approach was more hands-off than my mom's—higher expectations, more criticism, more responsibilities. In his day, many kids my age were getting married and taking over the farm. He wanted me to be ready for it all. I assumed his avoidance of a long goodbye was his way of saying, "I've done everything I can, I hope you prove me right."

My mom wiped her tears and said, "one more hug for the man who lights up my life."

It was my last childhood hug from my mother and she hugged me long and hard enough to last until my first visit home as an adult. It was then that we heard the horn honking on the car. As we peered out the window, we saw my dad standing outside of the car pressing on the horn anxious to get her out of there — and move my things to the basement.

I watched as my mom left my dorm and walked to our car. I saw her and my father embrace. And as they let go of one another, I saw them both brush tears from their faces. Maybe that is why my father couldn't say goodbye to me: he was afraid he'd cry, too. They had done all that they could. It was up to me now.

James *(38), Lawyer*

Where to Live?

For most young adults, college is the first time they will leave the nest and be independent. (Or nearly entirely independent; financial independence is usually another hurdle, arriving after graduation.) It's an extremely challenging time in most people's lives. Not only do you have to juggle college, but you have to begin managing your own life and all the challenges that come along with that. It's both exciting and terrifying. You probably spent the past four years struggling to be awarded more independence and suddenly, it's all yours. Given that this will be your first chance to spread those wings and take flight, it's important that you reflect on this major transition and be prepared for it. You will also need to be honest and self-aware about how ready you are to leave the nest because it's a long way to fall. Along with the many options for college, you also have a variety of options for determining where to live.

Most colleges and universities offer dormitories. These large, usually drab college fortresses offer all you will need shoved into a small space; enough room to sleep above where you will study and close enough to your roommate so that you can high five them from your bed each night. Some colleges require you to live on campus for a certain number of years, whereas other campuses barely have enough room for all of their freshmen.

Some colleges have quads, where you will live with four people and share a bathroom and living room, and other colleges have a concrete rectangular room for you that is just bigger than a prison cell. The dorms are a great place for you to be surrounded by multitudes of peers, a totally diverse student cohort all going through the same awkward transition. Some people meet the friends they will have for life in the dorms, and some even meet the partners they will eventually marry. The dorms are like a rite of passage and provide a way to ease into adulthood with just enough rules and policies to keep you safe, assuming you follow them, and a couple that will just irritate you. They are fun, overwhelming, exciting, but can get stifling and dull after a year or two.

You will need to carefully consider the advantages and disadvantages of dorm living before committing to living there and the options that may be available. First and foremost, many colleges don't allow you to pick your roommate. I'm sure you're thinking about being stuck with some really annoying, messy and stinky person, but you can bet that person is also worried about being stuck with you. Not everyone becomes best friends with their first college roommate, and in fact, most people don't. The bigger question is whether you can tolerate this person enough to live with them. Moreover, for those of you who are the most self-aware, will someone be able to tolerate you?

Most people roll the dice and get placed with a random person. This is always a great way for you to not only get to know someone new, but also to "network" by meeting their friends. If you are someone who has trouble getting along with people or the thought of submitting this process to chance is causing panic attacks, you can also see if the college will allow you to pick a roommate.

In this case, you can solicit a friend who is also attending the college, get a recommendation from friends or family who also know of someone attending the college, or search for someone on social media or other community boards. This will give you the chance to get to know someone before agreeing to live with them.

For some of you, and hopefully you know who you are, living with someone may just not be a great idea. This isn't a significant problem, there are plenty of ways to get to know people in college without living within arms' reach of them. If you have some rigidity in your living space or behaviors or habits that may be too much for a roommate, you may want to consider living on your own. Colleges often have an application process for getting a single room. A single can allow you to maintain your own space and sanity, while venturing out and meeting people in a more comfortable way. Generally, singles are hard to attain, but if you are starting college with a disability and you believe your disability is the primary reason you won't be successful living with someone, you are more likely to get this by applying for an accommodation.

For example, if you have obsessive/compulsive challenges and it's going to cause you (or a roommate) undue stress to have someone living in your space, the college may accommodate your disability. Similarly, if you have Autism and you know that your rigidity or need for stimming will make getting along with your roommate too challenging, then you may also be eligible for a single. Don't forget, this doesn't mean that you can't walk across the hall and meet like-minded friends, it just ensures that you have a safe space to return to.

After reading all of this, you may still be thinking that living in the dorm sounds horrible. Whether you know it will be too chaotic or are anticipating feeling trapped, the dorms are certainly not right for everyone. Not to worry, most college towns are packed full of low-income student housing. Although it will probably be more expensive than a dorm, you will have your own place without the daunting social complexities of a large college residence. Living in your own apartment means that you will be biting off a bit more to chew, so you have to be reflective on whether you are ready to take on college and also manage your own apartment, including bills, food, cleaning, and the like. However, this may be just the right oasis for you to escape to when college life becomes overwhelming.

A final option: there is no shame in living at home, and this strategy has become more common of late. There are numerous reasons why people live at home while going to college. For many, the cost of college and living is just too great, so living at home can ease the burden. For others, transitioning to independence while also attempting to be successful in college may just be too much. If you are choosing to attend a community or vocational college, there may be no dorms available, so home or an apartment is the only reasonable choice.

Conversely, living at home for some people may actually be inhibiting their growth and independence. It's important to be honest with yourself when making this decision and it's obviously important to talk it through with your parents. Will moving out help you practice a deeper independence or will you actually jeopardize your holistic independence by moving out of a consistent source of stability, support and convenience? Will taking classes while living at home for a year be a safer transition to college or are you just delaying it due to your anxiety? Will living at home add to the stress of college or relieve it? Will living at home make it easier or more difficult for you to be involved on campus? These are the questions that only you can honestly answer. Unfortunately, it may feel much more defeating and may prove to be more difficult to move back home once you have left, so you should be thoughtful in your consideration.

Roommate Relationships

Unless you shared a room with your sibling, or you have maintained a long-term relationship with your imaginary friend, for those of you who decide to live in a dorm or apartment with other students, this will be your first time sharing a small living and sleeping space. If college didn't provide enough challenges already, maintaining a positive relationship with your roommate(s) will take effort and attention. Giving your full effort to do well in school will require that you have a safe and comfortable space to return to and decompress. If college and your living situation are both stressful, you will be setting yourself up for failure.

Most people think that they are easy to live with, but the reality is that no one is easy to live with. The way you like things may be the way your roommate hates things. Your level of cleanliness may seem like a landfill to your roommate, and your roommate's organizational strategy may look like post-hurricane wreckage to you. Plus, everyone has that "button."

You have your own buttons, as well. Just think about the one thing that drives you crazy. It's likely that one or all of your roommates will do it daily. Will they leave the toilet seat up? Slurp their cereal? Snore? Leave their socks on the floor? Forget to feed their howler monkey? What may be worse is that you will also push your roommates' buttons. Not only will it be hard to remember not to push that button, but you will probably never understand why they care so much that you don't drink the milk after eating your cereal. So here are some important things to think about when developing a healthy relationship with your roommates.

Communicate

The first thing you should do with your roommate is talk openly with them about the expectations of your shared living space. Try to understand what they need to feel comfortable and be honest with what you will need. Setting up expectations early will save some unneeded frustration later and will also open up the lines of communication to solve inevitable problems in the future. Here are some questions worth exploring:

- *What space is mine, what space is yours? What ground rules are we both willing to abide for shared space?*
- *What are your quiet hours?*
- *What's our policy on having friends in our space?*
- *How should we deal with cleaning? Schedule? Daily?*
- *What are your pet peeves?*
- *What's your comfort level in borrowing one another's things?*
- *Do you want to share food or buy our own?*
- *When we have issues, what's the best way to bring them up with one another?*
- *How should we deal with paying common bills?*

Explore these questions with your roommate and share your preferences with them, as well. As you identify more points of contention with them over time, be up front and ask direct questions to solve the problem. Letting issues simmer will only bring them to a boil, and most problems are easily solved with simple openness. Check in with your roommate regularly and make sure *they* aren't letting any problems simmer. Genuinely try to hear feedback and do what you can to make their space comfortable and "home" again; this will also nurture their willingness to be respectful of your needs. Having a happy roommate will only add to the positive energy you will need to be successful in college.

Good Fences Make Good Neighbors

There will be three spaces in your living space: your space, your roommate's space and your shared space. Now imagine there is a fence between your space and their space. Your job is not to cross it. If you are a messy person, keep your mess to your own space. If you are a tidy person, just tidy your own space. Here is the big secret: the big problems begin when you start infringing on other people's space and the cramped quarters highlight the contrast even more.

For example, two college students were the polar opposites in cleanliness. One roommate was a neat-freak and the other was a total slob. They shared a small dorm room and the slob was constantly leaving his clothes and things all over the room. After months of fighting about it, the Dorm Supervisor came up with a very creative solution. He walked into their room with a roll of duct tape and made a line down the center of their room. He pointed at one side and said, "Messy" and pointed at the other side and said "Tidy," looked at the two of them and said, "don't cross the line." From that point forward, the tidy roommate kept his side the way he wanted it, and the slob kept all of his mess on his side of the line. They got along just fine from that day forward. Or more accurately, no one died. Don't worry, you probably don't need to pack duct tape, but you should think of your spaces as if they were sacred and respect your roommate's preference for how they want to live in their space. They should do the same for you.

Here's the hard part, your shared space will require compromise. This is the space where both sets of rules will have to apply. First off, it's shared space, "ours," which means that if you are the more slovenly, none of your disorganization can spill into "ours." The other rule of thumb is that the neater person sets the precedent.

If your roommate hates dirty dishes in the shared space, you will have to respect that and clean up after yourself. If you need that space to be cleaner than your roommate wants it, you will either have to open up the lines of communication and consistently make sure they know of your expectation, or if you don't mind, you'll have to make the effort at keeping the area clean. You should definitely have a schedule or strategy for organizing and cleaning the shared space. It could be as simple as every night you clean it up together or once a week you take turns cleaning your shared space. Regardless, this shared space will require that you are communicating with your roommate to be sure you are both comfortable in it.

Cleaning "mi casa, su casa"

Everyone likes a clean space but it takes work; the Second Law of Thermodynamics warns that nature insidiously slides toward disorder. Even if you can tolerate living in a messy room, you know that when you actually clean it you feel a little proud that you conquered entropy this day. While some folks claim "it's who they really are," most people don't clean simply because they are either lazy or they have a higher tolerance for chaos. And their parents have probably adapted around them.

No one likes sifting through a pile of clothes on a dirty floor to identify the least dirty shirt to wear that day. In college, you no longer have your parents forcing you to clean your room or doing it for you, but this is not a reason to let your space turn into a disaster zone. Moreover, regardless of the amount of duct tape you lay down on your dorm room floor, your roommate, your friends, and your roommate's friends will still be able to see how you live.

You want to communicate that you respect your space as much as you respect yourself. Come up with strategies that help you keep the entire space in great shape, at least once a week. Buy a hamper or clothes bin and immediately throw your dirty clothes into it or shove all of your clothes and random things into your closet and organize it weekly. Regardless, keeping your life in order starts at your new home; if you aren't going to clean and organize your whole and your half of "ours" daily, then at the very least set aside one day a week on your calendar to do it. Not only will you feel better, but your roommate will appreciate your efforts.

Making Nice With Your Roommate

There will undoubtedly be conflicts with your roommate. If you ever had a Betta fighting fish — those beautiful fish with flowing fins that you probably won at your local fair by tossing a ping pong into their small round tank — then you've witnessed what it's like to have a roommate. They're the epitome of territorialism. If you put two betta fish into a fish bowl together, they fight until the victor destroys the loser. However, if you put their bowls next one another, they swim in circles in harmony and only occasionally come face to face, at which time they puff up their fins and shake at one another until they realize they are both stuck in a circular hell and continue on their circular way.

You and your roommate are betta fish with your own private bedroom bowls, but co-habitating in the same bigger bowl. Every once in a while, you'll puff up your fins and shake them at one another. So, you need to plan for the fin shaking.

First and foremost, conflicts are more easily solved when you have established mutual respect. As you well know, relationships take work. Imagine your relationship as a piggy bank. When you first meet your roommate, the bank is empty. With every positive encounter and interaction, you begin to add value to your piggy bank. However, with each conflict, you take some value out of the piggy bank. If you resolve your conflict, you get back to even, if not adding some value back for strengthening the relationship through cooperation, mutual sacrifice and thereby resolving your differences.

Your first goal will be to add as much value as frequently as you can. Being a good roommate, like keeping your space clean and respecting your shared space, will be your regular deposits; think of this as investing the minimum wage. If you want to really start adding value, you'll need to go out of your way to do nice things and find times to do fun things together. Even if this person isn't going to end up being your best friend in the long run, finding some time to do things together is very important. It allows you to take a break from being roommates and be friends instead.

So, what can you do? The list is probably limitless and depends on your roommate, but here are some ideas:

- Get a meal together regularly. Standing lunch date once or twice a week in between classes? Hot wing night at the local pub? Picnic at the park?

- Do an activity together that you have shared interest in. Sports? Bowling? Knitting? Bird watching? Fish fighting?

- Buy them some small thing, occasionally. Cup of their favorite coffee? Pack of gum? Donut? Betta fish?

- Be willing to go out of your way for them. Give them a ride if they need one. Could you pick up their dry cleaning? Bring them the book they forgot at the library?

- Give them compliments. Hey I like your new shoes! Thanks for cleaning up! You're the best knitter I know! Cool new tattoo!

Even after adding tons of value to your proverbial piggy bank, you'll still need to take out some withdrawals occasionally, so hopefully you have made enough deposits. Conflict, arguments and fighting are healthy ways of maintaining a relationship. Not only is avoiding conflict unrealistic, it's also unhealthy. Resolving these conflicts successfully will actually result in making some very valuable deposits.

Here are some tips for successfully resolving your conflicts:

The problem is not the person. The problem is what the person is doing or has done. Instead of only pointing out the problem, focus on what you want changed. It will lead to less tension and conflict, and it is far less "personally" attacking. For example, if your roommate is often playing their music too loudly and preventing you from sleep or studying, saying "I want you to be less of a noisy rude jerk" will result in more conflict plus your roommate is still not sure what they can do to be less of a noisy rude jerk.

However, identifying that the problem is not with the person, but rather with the volume of the music will help you to solve the dispute. Think about what it is that you want changed, and make that the center of your request. Respectfully address your roommate the way you would like them to talk to you. Generally, "I statements" are the most effective.

The formula is fairly simply and can be used in any request: When you (state the problem), I feel (state how it makes you feel), because (state how it affects you), so I'm hoping you will (state how they can change).

For example, "when you play your music loudly, I feel frustrated because I can't concentrate on my reading, so I'm hoping you could turn your music down when I'm studying."

This assertive approach will increase the likelihood that you will get what you want out of the conflict. It provides a clear negotiation, and illuminates your experience for your roommate.

Healthy relationships involve constant compromise and planning, not just emotional honesty. Just because you want something to happen in a certain way and you've addressed it with an "I statement" doesn't mean you automatically get your way. Solving the problem may actually involve both of you making some changes. Focus on the problem and the solution that will make you both happy.

If your roommate needs loud music on to study, consider other ways you can accommodate one another. Can you set up certain times when they can play their music loudly? Can you both use headphones? Can you agree on a volume that works for both of you? By only accepting your solution, you create more conflict, when in reality there is usually more than one way to solve the problem.

Don't be defensive. Even if you perfect your "I statements", it doesn't mean that your roommate will use "I statements" when confronting you. Remember, the problem is not with either of you, it's with what one of you is doing. Therefore, bring it back to what needs to be changed for both of you to be happy. If your roommate confronts you and says, "You're a messy slob," take a deep breath and bring it back to the problem by interpreting their statement in a way that focuses on the problem and not the person, and then inquire about a potential solution.

"It sounds like you are frustrated with my cleanliness, is there something I can do to make it better?" Hear them out and find the compromise that works for both of you. Responding to them with the same attacking tone will only make things worse.

Talk about your feelings. For some people, this will be extremely tough; either this is an area that you are uncomfortable with or you have difficulties identifying your emotions. Regardless, it's important to let your roommate know that you are human and come with feelings and emotions. If you are upset about how they treated you, did something to make you feel sad, or embarrassed you, find a time to let them know how what they did made you feel. You don't need to be dramatic about it, and you probably don't need to have a long conversation about it, just letting them know will help them know how to treat you differently in the future. It can be as simple as an "I statement".

"Hey, when you called me a messy slob, I felt unappreciated because most of the time, I'm doing my best, so I'm hoping you would be more respectful to me in the future."

Problems are like raw fish. If you deal with them immediately, you can make delicious sushi. However, if you let them sit, they get stinkier and more rotten over time. Make sushi with your problems. Address them immediately and work toward compromise. Simple problems become more frustrating and difficult to deal with the longer you wait. If you smell rotten fish, seek out the source with your roommate and deal with the problem. Neither of you want to live in an environment that stinks of rotten fish.

Managing Your Limited Budget

No one likes the person who is always asking to borrow money, and especially not the person who never pays you back. Whether you were living on an allowance, regularly asking your parents for money, supporting yourself with a part time job, checking under couch cushions for change, or fortunate enough to have your parents' credit card, beginning to establish and live within a budget is mandatory for living independently. And, living a life of independence does impress your peers, job prospects, and folks who'll need your guidance. It is one of the hardest aspects of "maturing." But most people make budgeting way more complex than it needs to be. It boils down to simple addition and subtraction; what makes it difficult is commitment – the planning ahead and then the huge dose of self-discipline.

There is a clever dictum on many college and office walls: "discipline is just choosing between what you want now, and what you want most." You hopefully see the difference, regarding budgeting — here's how to respect it: let's say your budget allows you to spend $400 a month. First, you need to account for your regular expenses. Do you buy a cup of coffee every morning? Do you have a Netflix subscription? Do you and your roommate go out for lunch once a week? How much do you spend on groceries each month? These are the costs that you can accurately predict.

Second, think about the things that are more difficult to predict and guess what it might cost you. For example, how much you might need for school supplies or going to see movies. Add up those monthly survival costs (rent, groceries, internet, transport, phone, etc.), regular (aka "budgeted"!), social / living expenses (Netflix, pizza, ski pass) and subtract from your total, and what remains is your "disposable income", aka fun money. The only money you can spend in one month on fun things is your fun money. Budgeting, aka discipline, aka being grown up requires that you spend less than your entire disposable income every month on fun stuff.

How to do this? Plan monthly for the items or events that you know will come out of your fun money. So, if you know that you'll be going to a concert and this will cost you $50, you have $50 less fun money to spend that month. The good news is that if you don't spend all of your fun money, it rolls into the next month. Here's an example of a budget for the $400/month:

This Month's Budget - $400	
Daily coffee	$60
Netflix	$10
Groceries	$100

Weekly lunch	$80
Supplies	$50
Movies	$40
TOTAL EXPENSES	$340
Fun money	$60

Now that you know you have $60 to spend on fun things each month, your job will be to monitor each fun purchase you make - and subtract it from the month's budget. If you run through all the numbers and you are unhappy about how much fun money that you have, then you'll need to adjust your fixed costs. Can you spend less at the grocery store? Can you skip your weekly lunch? Can you buy a coffee maker and thereby save money over time? With each adjustment your fun money will increase, but you need to be realistic about where you can cut costs. At the end of every month, look at your bank statement and consider how you spent your money. You may need to either increase or decrease items on your budget. It's also possible that you realize that you need to budget for items that you forgot, like the daily fare on the bus. If that comes up, find out if your school provides student rate public transport passes? Cha-ching!

Modify your budget every month until it is as accurate as possible and then here's the really hard part — be disciplined about only spending the money that you have. This will sometimes take real sacrifice. If you know that you need to spend budgeted fun money on going to your concert and your friends invite you to go to a movie, then you'll have to decide which one you really want to do. Most importantly, don't spend money that you don't have. If at the end of the month it's time to pay your bills and you blew your money at the bowling alley, you have created financial consequences that snowball into your budget the next month. And remember that there are unexpected expenses — if you do need to tap into your next month's budget, be sure to adjust so that it doesn't become a recurring problem.

So, we should talk about credit cards. There are three important rules about credit cards.

1) Don't get a credit card.

2) If you get a credit card, be sure you can pay it off EVERY month.

3) If you can't pay it off every month, refer to rule #1.

There is this insane myth that somehow if you don't have a credit card in college, you can't start building credit and you'll be at a disadvantage when you graduate college. This advice could only have been made by credit card companies. They are hoping you will risk contracting for a credit card, max out your credit line, and then spend your young adulthood paying them insane amounts of interest back to make amends for your impulses in college. It's just not worth it, especially if you aren't extremely disciplined in only spending the amount you earn each month. There are very few people on the planet who have that ability. There are plenty of ways to build your credit over time, including buying a car, paying your bills on time, and waiting until you are making a salary and can afford a credit card.

Credit cards and drugs leverage a very dangerous part of the human brain, our reward centers; each must be treated with great deference, because short-term choices can have devastating consequences. Here's a classic mistake college students make - all of your friends are going to New Orleans for Spring Break. You don't have that kind of savings; you didn't budget for it and therefore can't afford it. But, as you are walking across campus, some enthusiastic person standing in front of a credit card advertisement asks if you want a hat for signing up for a credit card.

You think to yourself, "Wow! I could get a free hat and float the cost for my Spring Break." You figure you could just use the credit card for the flight and hotel room then just pay it off afterwards. So, you get the hat and the credit card and book your hotel and tickets.

When you get to New Orleans, someone says, "Hey, do you mind if we put groceries on your new fancy credit card, and we'll just give you cash." You think, "free cash? Of course." Then you spend the cash on things you wouldn't have bought otherwise, because it's *free cash*. Later that week when everyone is talking about doing a really cool swamp tour on an airboat, you say "yes," because you can charge it. What's another $100 after already having spent $750 thus far. When you get home, it feels like you had a free vacation.

Then the credit card bill comes.

Turns out that you charged $5000 on your whole vacation, which means you have a minimum payment of $200 covering the ungodly interest rate. No worries, it will only take you TEN years to pay that back. You will have paid the credit card company more than $3500 for loaning you the money to go on Spring Break for one week, plus the $5000 your borrowed. Your New Orleans Spring Break just cost you $8500, and for the next few years half of your monthly budget will now go to the credit card company, and most definitely not your fun money.

Do not get a credit card! In terms of impulsivity, craving and immediate cost, a credit card can be very much like experimenting with heroin, which, let's be clear, you shouldn't do either.

Finally, there are a plethora of great budgeting tools that you can use to help make your life easier. There are apps that help you keep track of your expenses and most banks even offer their own apps to help you keep track of your spending and budget. Third party applications like Mint can be connected directly to your bank account and can help you make a monthly budget, track your expenses, give you warnings when your funds are running low, and help you categorize where you spent your money. The programs are only as good as the user's discipline, so you have to monitor the app frequently and make wise decisions based on what the app is telling you. These programs will help you do just about everything financially, but they won't tame your impulses to buy something when you can't afford it. You need to be the one making wise financial decisions – including declining the credit card in the first place!

Healthy Eating: Preserving Your Natural Advantages

Do you remember the days when your mom or dad would ask you what you wanted for dinner and you would say, let's order pizza or something else equally as delicious? Then they would usually say no before cooking you something that was relatively boring and simple with some vegetables… maybe a piece of chicken, white rice, and broccoli. You would daydream about the day when you could order pizza whenever you wanted and never eat your vegetables.

Well, that day has arrived. No one is going to be looking over your shoulder as you inhale pieces of greasy pizza, mounds of French fries, and extra helpings of delicious chocolate cake. You can eat Doritos for breakfast, twinkies for lunch, and chocolate chip pancakes for dinner. They have a name for this unbridled gluttonous phenomenon. They call it the dreaded "Freshman Fifteen." This phenomenon is when your toned adolescent body begins to stretch at the seams and your high school gym shorts begin to look like bike shorts, as you add fifteen pounds to your waistline.

It is true that with independence comes a seductive buffet of sugar and carbohydrates. And unbridled independence can morph you into a junk food junkie. The saying "you are what you eat" becomes more true as you enter adulthood. Like every other transition to independence, you will be the master (or victim) of your choices and what you choose to eat will be equally as important. To be clear, this is not about weight, per se, although this can be an unintended consequence of unhealthy eating; this is about health, discipline, restraint and giving your body the nutrients and fuel it needs to conquer all of your goals. Fueling your body to improve your mood, improve your concentration and sleep and fortifying your self-regard will be essential to leading a healthy and successful college life.

If you are lucky enough to have access to the college dining hall, then you will have the opportunity to have three well-balanced meals a day. However, you will also have the option to have seven unrestricted, unhealthy and artery-clogging meals a day. Indeed, dining halls across the country have moved to provide more healthy options for college students, mostly driven by consumers who desire a healthy diet. But those wonderful lunch ladies love to fatten up their sweet college kiddos and they aren't going down without a fight. In between the quinoa wraps and the kale soufflé, they have strategically placed pepperoni pizza with a cheese-filled crust wrapped in pieces of extra fatty bacon to tempt you to stretch your waistline. This very difficult choice will be yours alone, so you must use self-restraint with some careful planning to avoid their greasy trap.

First off, let's start with the good news. It's okay to eat unhealthy food occasionally. In fact, if you have some savory vices, then you should not live in denial about it and plan to indulge occasionally. Like intentionally including "fun money" in a healthy budget, your healthy eating plan should start with when and how often you are going to eat unhealthy food. If you love pizza, for example, decide when and how many times a week you'll allow yourself to eat it. But if your plan is to eat pizza every dinner, seven times a week, then you'll want to think about how you might cut that down to a reasonable amount.

Let's say you decide that you will limit eating pizza and/or other unhealthy food (hot wings, cheeseburgers, pasta alfredo, Chinese take-out) to only three meals a week. It will then be your goal to eat as healthy as possible for all of the other meals. This doesn't mean you have to eat lettuce wraps and steamed carrots for every meal, just think healthy. Get a turkey sandwich, but skip the bacon. Get some eggs and toast, and have one piece of sausage instead of two. Try the kale soufflé.

The four most beautiful and deadly words known to college students are "all you can eat." College cafeterias generally have an all you can eat policy. It is more accurately "all you care to eat." You should care to eat as much food as you need to be nourished and pleasantly full.

It won't be easy.

It's like a series of delightful surprises as you slowly move your tray down the line. Ooh, pasta marinara? I'll take just a little. Tater tots? Why not? Mozzarella sticks? Don't mind if I do. Cheeseburger? Put it on top of the tots.

So, what's the solution? Take one plate of food, no seconds, and no stacking. One full plate of food is absolutely all you need to eat to be healthy and full. It doesn't matter how much healthy food you have on your plate, if you eat three plates of it. Use self-control to limit the amount of food you take. It won't be easy, but your heart will thank you.

If you are fixing your own meals, possibly even "brown-bagging" your lunches to campus, here are some very simple nutrition guidelines: some carbs, some protein (yogurt has protein!), a serving of vegetables if practical, some fruit and probably some other sugars as a treat, and a midday snack. A good spectrum of nutrition provides your metabolism with fuel throughout the day's usage. The brain requires a continual supply of blood-borne glucose, so… eat a good snack midday to remain alert, and sharp.

Whenever practical, eat with friends. It's good for your soul, and it stops you from shoveling food mindlessly. This is especially true if the present circumstances in school are discouraging you. Talking more and eating less is definitely better for you.

Now, for those of you who do not have the luxury, or better yet, the food binge temptation Hell that is a cafeteria, cooking at home is a great opportunity to save money and eat healthy. Eating out every single meal is not only expensive, but generally, restaurants make their food delicious by making it extremely unhealthy.

For example, let's say that you decide to skip the burger for the day and instead order a chicken pot pie from KFC. Sounds delicious and nutritious, right? But this isn't your mom's chicken pot pie. That specific pot pie has the equivalent of 74 chicken wings worth of saturated fat.[11] Additionally, the one pot pie provides you with almost your entire day's recommended intake of salt, fat, and calories. This is not a super food, instead it's a pie with a surprise heart attack inside. Cooking a chicken pot pie at home will provide you with something just as delicious for less than half the price, and nutritionally, twice as good for you.

The trick to cooking at home is shopping regularly, and practice (learn from your mistakes). Add your weekly or bi-weekly shopping trip to both your calendar and your budget. Before heading to the car, plan what meals you want to cook for the week and create a shopping list of items that you will need to purchase. Do not go to the grocery store without a list

---

11 (http://blog.paleohacks.com/worst-fast-food/#)

and definitely do not go to the grocery store without a list when you are hungry. Items that you make will always be healthier and less expensive than items you heat up. So, think about getting mostly whole ingredients, while adding some frozen items to microwave or heat up when you are running late or don't feel like cooking.

You should spend the majority of your time in the produce section. It's usually the first place you walk through when entering a grocery story. Fresh foods are always better for you. If you have the funds, try to purchase items that are organic, as they will be free of the preservatives and saturated fats that will clog your arteries. Force yourself to choose the healthier options when you have a choice.

Avoid the frozen foods section, unless you are buying vegetables, but if you have to, look for the products that tout their healthiness. By title alone, you could probably determine that a Hungry Man lasagna is less healthy than Healthy Choice lasagna. Neither will taste as good or be as good for you as just looking up a recipe and making your own lasagna, which honestly isn't that hard.

Canned food, with lots of salt to make it taste 'fresher', can be extremely long-lived, which is why grocery stores prefer to stock and advertise them. But much like with frozen items, there are some less healthy hidden costs in there. Read the label, and keep an eye on portion size. That can of Chef Boyardee may look like it has reasonable calorie costs, but if it turns out that there are three and a half servings in a can... well, you're in college now — you can do the math.

Cooking is not rocket science, but it does take some practice. Not every meal that you try will come out perfect, but experience will improve it for the next time you make it. Most grocery items come with some handy instructions printed directly on the box; if the printed recipe sounds delicious, follow those! See how easy cooking can be?

For example, a box of spaghetti noodles says to bring 4 quarts of water to boil in a large pot, add a tablespoon of salt, add noodles, and cook 8-10 minutes until the noodles are soft, drain water, and rinse noodles with cold water. Follow those directions exactly the first time and see how they came out.

If your noodles were too soft or hard, your pot was too small, or you burned your hand when draining the noodles, adjust your strategy the next time you make pasta. This goes for everything you cook, try it out and adjust the next time.

Invite friends to help cook! Learning alongside someone who has some skill makes a better meal, and gives you both something healthy and inspirational to enjoy, is a great way to strengthen relationships, and maybe they'll even split the shopping bill.

Take-Aways:

- Be honest about the best living arrangement for you to maximize your success.
- Communicate openly, clearly, and regularly with your fellow betta fish.
- You are what you eat, so eat well.
- Budget for the fun stuff.

CHAPTER 15:

How to Engage

"For those of you who are always seeming to be stuck in the mud, would you please live a little? It's college for crying out loud and there will be plenty of time to read and be boring later in your life."

---

*D*o *you remember that scene in the first Star Wars when Luke, C-3PO, and Obi Wan walk into the Cantina and there are all of those strange aliens or creatures hanging around the bar? That's how my first day in college felt.*

I went to a huge state school, but came from a fairly small, quaint, rural town full of hicks and cornfields. I was definitely the black sheep of my high school. I was more liberal than most, liked science fiction instead of football, and preferred classical music over death metal. I had a small group of close friends, but tried to fly under the radar whenever possible. This wasn't helped by my Freshman year gym teacher calling me Lilac one day. That nickname stuck with all of the jocks. So basically, I was either hanging with my nerdy friends playing Dungeons and Dragons or being called Lilac in the locker room by smelly meatheads — that sums up high school for me, pretty much. You can imagine I was pretty psyched to get the hell out of there.

I think what most excited me about college wasn't that I could "start over," but I could start the way I wanted. I wasn't ever unhappy with me in high school, but it was other people's opinions of me that seemed to get in my way. I saw college as my opportunity to own who I am in the relative safety and freedom of an open-minded campus. I was basically excited to let my nerd flag fly and find others who wanted to join the club.

The first week of college was uneventful and awkward. My roommate was nice, but he was mostly looking forward to finding, as he put it, "beers and babes" in college. And everyone else in my dorm just seemed to be acting strangely: in trying to appear sincere and confident, everyone was working too hard to present themselves. I suppose I was guilty of it too. I had laid out a different sarcastic t-shirt to wear for each of the first five days of college, including my "Ask me if I care" t-shirt that I wore on the first day.

I honestly started to panic that I wasn't going to find my crew. I kept recalling the scene where Obi Wan and Luke keep going up to different aliens and then one tries to kill them so Obi Wan cuts his arm off. The college community seemed sort of scary, like that. I'd try out all of these different groups in the cafeteria or people sitting outside on the lawn and I always left feeling different, sort of like in high school.

During the second week of college and under some feeling of desperation, I saw a poster for Cult Movie night. It was happening on a Friday night at 9pm, so clearly my roommate would be preoccupied with babes and beer. I decided to go on my own. I was a huge fan of cult movies and quite honestly didn't want to sit alone in my room. I walked across campus to the Student Union, where there would be free pizza before the movie.

I nervously walked up to the door and hesitated before I opened it. Do you know in those movie scenes where someone opens a door to heaven, and that light shines through the door? My experience was like that, but instead of there being heaven on the other side, it was just a room full of nerds. Nerds just like me! I met many of the people who would become my crew in college that night. Two of them eventually stood up in my wedding, later in life. My crew had always been there, they had just been hiding, just like I had been, and I had to have the courage to go find them.

A few months after that night at the movies, I had everything I was looking for in college. People who liked me for who I am and didn't judge me. I found safety in being who I wanted to be without having to look over my shoulder. And that was all confirmed one night when I was walking with my crew down the street. I saw a guy I knew from high school, a locker room meathead, walking toward us. My stomach immediately dropped. I averted my gaze as he walked toward us, but as he walked by us, he looked at me and said aggressively, "Hey Lilac", then chuckled and kept walking. I felt really stupid, until one of my new friends exclaimed, "how'd that ogre get here from Mordor?" We all laughed and I realized I had found my place.

Michael *(42), English Professor*

Melding with the College Culture

Although the culture on every college campus is different, there seems to be an attitude shift in college that is similar across campuses. Whereas high school was often a time of exclusivity, popularity, and cliques, college becomes a more open-minded and inclusive environment. For many of you, I'm sure that this is welcome news. Now does this clique-culture still exist in college? It does, but in college you choose to participate in it or not.

There is still homecoming court in college, but the exclusivity and popularity contests are usually contained within the Greek (fraternity and sorority culture). However, if you make the choice that these things are not right for you, you won't be excluded. Instead, you'll just join the majority of people in college who would prefer to do their own thing and avoid the cool kid rat race. Quite simply, college is a place where you can finally let out a deep breath and just be yourself.

In fact, this paradigm of open-mindedness, respect for others' opinions, and a value of diversity is sort of the hallmark of a great college milieu. Often, people say that the most important thing that you learn in college is the ability to think. Critical thinking skills involve the ability to consider multiple perspectives in lieu of your own personal biases. Thus, being surrounded by people who are different is essential for the development of these skills. Not only will your viewpoints, perspectives, and individual expression be valued, but you will also begin to expand your worldview and reciprocate in your acceptance of others. College is not only a time to find yourself, it's also a time to discover the world of everyone else.

When you ask a group of parents to write down their best memory in college, not one parent ever writes anything about what they learned. Even though your parents likely want your best memory to be about your classes, they would never write that their best memory was the excitement and joy of learning about the Krebs Cycle in their biology class. Instead, they list memories of events and times that were fun. Things they did with other people and the joy it brought them.

When asked what he would have changed about his brief stint as a student at Harvard, Bill Gates responded, "Well, I wish I would have been more sociable. I wish I had gotten to know more people. I was just so into being good at the classes and taking lots of classes." College is a time for fun. It has to be. There is no way to manage the stress and pressure of earning a college degree without the ability to go out with some friends and blow off some steam. It is so essential to have fun in college that you need to plan on how to have fun. And, if you are not having fun in college, it is essential you figure out what you are doing wrong, and fix it.

Obviously, fun is different for everyone. Fortunately, most colleges have a plethora of fun things to do for all different kinds of people. The important thing is that you seek out those things and commit yourself to doing them. Whether you want to play sports, do outdoor activities, write poetry, solve math equations, make baskets, or hit people with fake medieval swords, you will likely find your passion. What's even better about finding your passion is that it will usually lead you to other people who have similar passions and mindsets. There's nothing surprising about the fact that if you join the Quidditch club, you will probably find a bunch of similar Harry Potter nerds who will gladly run around with you with a broomstick between your legs. The point of the matter is that YOUR people are out there, you just need to go and find them.

There Are Clubs and Activities for EXACTLY Your Type of People

So where do you find these clubs and activities? Generally, most colleges have a list of clubs and activities on their website or in a catalog. This will usually list when and where the club meets or how to contact them. Most colleges have some version of a Club Fair at the beginning of the semester, where they invite all of the social organizations on campus to come to an event space. Yes, they are trying to recruit you to join them. This will allow you to see all the different clubs on campus and talk to someone who is already involved in it. This will give you a sense if the club and the people in the club are right for you.

The next step will be for you to actually attend the club. This may seem daunting, but keep in mind, the ones who have already been there want you to join the club, and everyone else is new, and just as scared as you are. They created the club so that people like you would have something fun to do and if you didn't join them, they wouldn't be able to do it. So as awkward as your first attendance may feel, it will feel better once you get to know the members and you begin having fun together. If you have a like-minded friend on campus, attending the club together will make it less awkward and easier to attend that first meeting. Regardless, take the leap and try it out.

Drinking and Drugs: A Real, Tragic Risk

For many people, the idea of having fun in college is getting wasted. There is no doubt that the media and popular culture propagates the idea that college is about binge drinking, streaking, and smoking weed. There is, also, no doubt that these activities will be available, on the campus you attend. But what's also true is that the majority of students in college do not binge drink. Over 40% of college students don't drink at all[12]. So, although you may be expecting a beer fest when you attend college, if that's not your thing, there will be plenty of people around you who feel the same way. You do not need to get wasted to find your people and have fun. In fact, these are probably the people you will want to avoid.

Quite frankly, if you are reading this book, you probably have enough to deal without adding alcohol and drugs to the mix. You need every brain cell, every ounce of attention, and every iota of processing speed to be successful in college. Drinking and drugs will not make your scholastic life any easier. In fact, 25% of students who drink regularly experience negative academic consequences and binge drinkers are six times more likely to do poorly in class[13]. Moreover, (before the coronavirus pandemic), there were over 1800 deaths in college related to drinking every year, almost 700,000 assaults, and almost 100,000 cases of sexual assault reported each year related to drinking. So, these are all great reasons to stay away from it.

Okay, so now to the readers who are going to do it anyway. Rather than taking the DARE approach of preaching fear and abstinence, hopefully we can be more honest and realistic about drinking and drugs. First, if you are under 21 and choose to drink or smoke marijuana in a state where it's not legal, you open yourself up to a ton of legal and campus violations that may make your life extremely complicated and lead to expulsion

---

12   National Institute on Alcohol Abuse and Alcoholism
13   National Institute on Alcohol Abuse and Alcoholism

from your campus. That's not to say that you won't be surrounded by other people who will gladly ignore these regulations and take the risk.

So, don't take the risk, that's the easiest advice.

If you take the risk, let's be realistic. The vast majority of people who choose to drink alcohol or smoke weed, do so responsibly. If you are someone who would like to drink or smoke weed and is able to do so responsibly, then monitoring your usage and performance in college will be crucial. If your grades and class performance begin to suffer because of your drinking or smoking, you'll need to draw limits around your use. This may involve choosing what you need to get done before having your glass of wine, or limiting your use entirely to weekends. Regardless, it'll be up to you to be sure that it's not getting in the way of your success in college.

If you can't regulate your use, then you join a large population of people who likely shouldn't drink or use drugs and you need to find the support to stop your usage. Keep in mind, while many people in college don't drink at all, some of your cohort have successfully stopped after developing a problem So, people with similar substance abuse needs are out there. The most important thing will be for you to be honest with yourself. You know whether you are losing the argument with that voice in your head telling you to take a hit or have another drink. Only you know if your binge drinking is leading you to fail your classes and lose friends. You need to be the one who recognizes that getting high in the morning is creating more problems than the "medicinal effects" you use to justify it. If you need help, then college campuses have a ton of great resources to help you quit. Go to the counseling center, if you haven't already, and talk with them about your usage. Even if you think you will be kicked out of the drinking club, know that there is a much healthier and more productive club of great people who share in your difficulty to regulate drinking and drugs.

Remember, you are already going to battle with your diverse learning needs to follow your dreams. Don't let drugs and alcohol be what defeats you.

Dating

Because you will be surrounded by like-minded people and can finally be yourself, many people meet their future partner in college. College is a great time to begin dating, if you haven't already started. For those Cool Jane's and Joe's out there who don't need any dating advice, feel free to skim ahead. For the rest of us who find or have found dating to be awkward, terrifying, confusing or non-existent, having a conversation about it may be worthwhile.

Finding a boyfriend or girlfriend can be one of the most befuddling processes in life, though it doesn't need to be. Granted, there will be moments of awkwardness and heartbreak, but this isn't any different than other aspects of your life. Dating should be fun and finding someone who you enjoy spending time with will be worth your efforts.

So, how do you start the process of dating? Dating is no different than building a friendship. In fact, all good partnerships start with friendship first. Unlike elementary school when you could send someone a note with the question "Will you be my boyfriend?" with a "yes or no" option, healthy dating in the adult world begins with someone who is your friend. Whether you meet them in class, at a party, or via an online dating site, they should be a friend. Often, attraction happens in the beginning of your friendship, but it can also be the result of your friendship.

If you find someone on campus attractive and you begin to build a friendship with them, it may lead to romance. However, you may have a friend on campus who over time you begin to find attractive *because* of your friendship. Either way, building the friendship is the foundation.

Once you've identified someone who you think may be a future romantic partner, you need to build your friendship. Honestly, this is a much less terrifying concept than dating them. Instead of asking if they want to share a single spaghetti noodle with you, find out what you may have in common and see if they would be interested in doing that with you.

If you discover you both love long walks on the beach, ask if they want to join you for a long walk on the beach. Again, participating in the Long Walks on the Beach Club at your college makes finding someone much easier. Regardless, healthy romantic relationships will only, and can only, come after you've built a positive friendship with that person. So, focusing your efforts on being their friend initially will be more successful than trying to first be their boyfriend or girlfriend.

Your potential future romantic partner could be just about anywhere, but this mysterious creature most likely lurks in the corners you also most frequently haunt. Thus, getting involved with activities and clubs on campus will expose you to the potential friendships that may turn romantic. If those corners of your life aren't fruitful, then people who you share similar viewpoints with in class or seem to have similar interests may lead to a friendship.

Finally, if you are still coming up empty-handed and really want to get dating, then you could consider an online dating website. The reputable websites will allow you to search for people with similar interests and chat with them online before having to meet them in person. This can save some awkwardness of meeting someone who you have nothing in common with. However, be sure that your first meeting is always in public and not some dark alley. Let's face it, there are a lot of creepy people out there.

There are only two words you need to familiarize yourself with when beginning to date — "yes" and "no." If you are interested in doing an activity with someone who you have some interest in and you ask them, they will respond with either a yes or a no; a maybe qualifies as no for all intents and purposes. Your response and future behavior must be dictated by that answer.

If they say yes, I'd like to go on a long walk on the beach with you, that is what they are willing to do until you ask them the next question. If they say no, this is most likely not a future match for you. Either you need to continue to build your friendship in other ways, or you need to move on. No *doesn't* mean keep trying, that's mostly for fictional romantic movies and love stories in cheesy books. In fact, not taking no for an answer usually qualifies you as a stalker, and this is not a reputation you want as you start your dating life.

The yes's and no's continue throughout your friendship and into your potential romantic relationship. You cannot assume anything without a direct answer to your question, especially if your relationship turns intimate. You need to ask permission to hold hands, put your arm around them, kiss them, and everything beyond. Without a yes or no, the answer is always no. And, no *always* means no. If you don't honor that answer then you are violating your partner. It is safest to ask the question and ask it numerous times to be sure you still have permission. This may seem embarrassing in some situations. It might seem unnecessary to you. But it is important. This is a rule that you seriously need to follow.

If you are in a relationship and your no's are not being respected, then you must talk to someone about it immediately. If they are not accepting no from you, then they won't accept no from other people in the future. If you are in a relationship and feel like you are not being respected like a friend or are being asked to do things emotionally or physically that you are not comfortable with, it is up to you to say no and end that relationship. If you are unsure about this, then talk to your friend, counselor, or professor, and allow them to help you understand your relationship.

Thousands of people are sexually assaulted on college campuses each year, and in many cases, it is by someone who is in a relationship with that person. As much as you need to respect yes and no in your relationships, it's as important that others are giving you the same respect. If they are not, it is essential that you end it immediately, and if you cannot, talk to someone to make it stop and stop that person from continuing the disrespect in the future. You deserve to be respected.

A quick word about sexual health. If you are a firm believer in abstinence, you can skim ahead. However, if you are sexually active or plan to be (and contrary to popular belief, many college students are not) then practice safe sex. If you are a sexually active male, always use a condom — even if your partner is a woman on birth control. If you are a heterosexual woman, and are sexually active, have condoms and require partners to use them; sexually transmitted diseases are rampant on college campuses. You may also want to consider an oral contraceptive (e.g., the pill) —

condoms are not 100% effective at preventing pregnancy. Overcoming a learning disability in college will be challenge enough, without also chasing a toddler around. Many college health centers will provide free condoms or very inexpensive birth control options. They are also there to talk with you more about this issue if you are open to it.

Finally, for some students, college is a time when they begin to explore their sexual and gender identities. This can include experimenting or identifying across a broad spectrum of gender identities or sexualities. Some may choose to disclose their sexual/gender identity while others may choose to keep this private. College will expose you to a wide range of individuals. Maturely respecting the diversity of others, while being honest with yourself about your own values and decisions, is an important practice in college life. There are plenty of resources and groups on most college campuses to help you navigate your sexual/gender identity and even more people experiencing this same journey. In the current day and age, there is no reason to hide who you are and who you love. Love is love.

Mastering a Work/Life Balance

One of the most important objectives you will have in college is mastering the work/life balance. For many people, this suggests that they will need to be sure not to have too much fun and to be sure they are being cognizant of their studies. Yes, obviously, this aspect of work/life balance is extremely important. However, for others this implies just the opposite. How will you inject more fun into your life to balance out the hard work that you are doing in college? You can't make it in college if you are having too much fun and equally as important, you can't make it in college if you don't have any fun. So, you'll need to figure out what end of the teeter totter that you ride on. Are you on the side that's always bumping into the ground or on the side that's always in the clouds? You're going to need a mix of both.

For those who need to come down from the clouds and have a little less fun, you'll need to figure out how to stay on top of your studies. Fortunately, if fun is not a problem for you, then rewarding yourself with it should be easy. Be smart about maintaining a schedule and reserving times for studying. View your work in school as uninterruptible by your fun, prioritize it, and don't compromise. There will always be something fun to do, so if you need to miss tonight's fun to finish that paper or study for that test, tomorrow night's fun will be even better. Use your fun activities as rewards. Schedule fun things to do once you've completed the mundane school work that you are dreading. No matter what, don't let the fun of college overcome the point of college. If you fail out because of the fun you are having, your fun will go away. Find the correct balance to manage both.

For those of you who are always seeming to be stuck in the mud, would you please live a little? It's college for crying out loud and there will be plenty of time to read and be boring later in your life. This is a time in your life that you will never get back and if you don't use it well, you'll spend the rest of your life wishing you could. More importantly, you need fun in your life to balance the stress and anxiety that college will bring. Isolating and hiding in your dorm room will only perpetuate your social anxiety and depression. You need to get out there and find the activities that will bring you joy in the company of others. Granted, you may never be the social butterfly that you see on the other side of the teeter totter and may never need to be reminded to be less social, but you need to create that outlet.

Your people are out there. But you need to take the initiative to go and find them. If you are down on life and overwhelmed by school, putting the books to the side for a day and doing something you love with people you enjoy is possibly the only solution there will be to building your motivation to keep going forward. We need people in our lives and college is a great opportunity to find them.

Take-Aways:

- Your people are out there, you just need to go out and find them.
- You need to balance the work and fun in your life.
- Relationships begin with and grow from friendships.

CHAPTER 16:

Get to Work, Literally

"Vocational skills go much deeper than just the knowledge needed for your line of work; they also involve using that knowledge in a workplace environment."

"*Today is the day I am going to be taken seriously.*" I remember repeating that to myself as I attempted to tie my dad's tie around my neck for the fifteenth straight time watching a YouTube instructional video on my phone. Too long one time, too short the next, wrong shape altogether most of the times.

When I first said I wanted to attend college, my guidance counselor literally said, "That's cute." I had been diagnosed with Asperger's Syndrome at a young age, so I spent the majority of school in and out of "special classrooms." It wasn't that I was stupid, it was that I learned so differently from how my teachers were teaching, that apparently, I needed a different classroom altogether. I don't think anyone believed *that I would be capable of attending college, including myself. That was until I had a teacher in high school who would always say that everyone has two qualities — strengths and areas for potential strength. When he asked me what I wanted to do after high school and I said go to college, he asked what I wanted to major in. It was the first time someone looked me dead in the eye and took me seriously. I told him that I wanted to be a lawyer, to which he responded, "maybe you can teach them some social skills." He was kidding of course, but it was from that day forward that I was set on being a lawyer.*

I thought my college classes were mostly easy. I hated anything to do with math or science, but was able to struggle through those with some help from a team of tutors at the college. My hope was to graduate with the best GPA I could manage and then apply to law school, but I also knew that my senior year internship placement would be crucial for me to get into a good law school. Even throughout college, I didn't feel like people were taking me seriously about wanting to be a lawyer. I'm sure it was because of my general social discomfort, lack of eye contact, or quite possibly the fact that I hated getting dressed up so I was often found wearing sweatpants and a t-shirt. I certainly didn't come off as the lawyer type. Nevertheless, I loved case law and reading briefs. I knew I would be a great lawyer, maybe not the front of the courtroom trial lawyer, but the guy who can find every loophole from the back office.

The senior internships were really competitive. I was at a huge disadvantage given my disability. I was not good at interviewing and I was definitely not the prototypical internship candidate. There was one particular law firm that had some internships available and I was told it was a difficult placement to get. I needed that placement. I applied for the internship and was given a time to come in and interview. Honestly, I almost decided to give up right away, especially knowing the other students I would be up against. But instead, I decided I'd lay everything on the table.

The interview was fairly painful. I struggled through most of the questions, not in the content of my answers, but in my ability to express them effectively. I could tell that I was making the other people in the room as uncomfortable as I was feeling. After about fifteen minutes, they asked me if there was anything I would like to say before ending the interview. At first, I shook my head, but as I remembered everything that I had gone through to be sitting in this seat at this moment, I spoke up and said, "Obviously, you can tell I'm different. Probably much different than all the other candidates who have or will walk through this door. I have Asperger's Syndrome, but that's only one of my great strengths. I am obsessed with the law. I read case studies in my spare time and my favorite place to take a date, if I ever get one, would be the law library. My strengths are my ability to be completely absorbed by my work and although I may not be the guy who everyone will want to grab a drink with, I'm the guy who everyone will trust to get the job done. I've never wanted anything more in my life and if you give me this opportunity, I will work every day to share my strengths and continue to develop my potential strengths each and every day."

And then I walked out of the room, only to remember that I forgot to shake everyone's hand, so I walked back into the room and shook each person's hand. It was slightly awkward, but at this point, it didn't matter. It was the best that I could do. I received a call a week later from the firm and they asked me if I would like to join them for my internship experience. I didn't hesitate to say yes.

After I finally got that tie just right, I put on the sport coat that my dad had given me a few years earlier and left my dorm room for my first day of internship. As I walked down the hallway, several people gave me compliments on how professional I looked, especially considering my baseline was sweatpants. I felt prouder of myself on that day than any day in my life up to that point. I felt this unusual swagger in my step and my chin seemed to be higher than it had ever been. Today was going to be the day that people were going to take me seriously.

David *(23), Law Student*

Developing Vocational Skills

As you've probably noticed, there is a lot to balance in college to be successful. If you weren't already fretting at the need to balance your academics, with your independent living, and your social life, there's a final equally-as-important domain you will need to balance to fully get the most out college — building your employability skills.

This probably sounds more daunting than it is, but college is a time when you not only begin to learn the skills that you will need for future career but also a time when you begin to practice those skills. Students who leave college with both cutting-edge knowledge of their career and work experience within their career will be the first in line to get the good jobs. There are plenty of ways to build your resume in college to get you that coveted job interview, you just need to balance it with everything else you are doing.

So, what are vocational skills? I'm sure you've heard this phrase throughout high school and have been told you need to develop them. Simply put, vocational skills are the skills you need to be successful in a particular trade or profession. Accordingly, if you want to be a computer programmer, your vocational skills include keyboard and typing, basic computer languages, some orientation around Command Line interface - the skills you need to program computers. But anyone who has worked anywhere in tech, or elsewhere, will tell you, hard skills are barely half the battle.

Vocational skills go much deeper than just the knowledge needed for your line of work; they also involve using that knowledge in a workplace environment. Vocational skills include the skills needed for your line of work, but also finding a job, marketing yourself, working with other people, following through on responsibilities, being on time, solving conflicts, finding work/life balance, and the list could go on. Fortunately, there are a variety of ways you can develop your vocational skills throughout college.

For those of you who have a documented disability, one thing you may want to consider is utilizing the services of your local Vocational Rehabilitation office, or what most people call Voc Rehab. Voc Rehab is a government-sponsored initiative to help adults with various disabilities to develop positive vocational skills, through job placements and on the job training. Voc Rehab offices often have numerous employment opportunities with employers who are interested in working with diverse learners. This is a great opportunity to develop your vocational skills with the support of experts who want to see you succeed. Contact your local Voc Rehab office to find out if qualify and to evaluate if it might be a good fit.

Volunteering Helps You Stand Out

Most successful college students volunteer regularly. With everything else on your plate, I'm sure you are questioning how adding a job that doesn't pay you any money makes any sense whatsoever. Well, volunteering is the gift that keeps on giving. There are a variety of benefits of volunteering, and not just in the ability to add it to your resume. When most people begin volunteering, they view the activity as giving selflessly to others. But as they continue in their experience, they begin to have this proverbial conflict regarding altruism and whether volunteering is truly a selfless act. That's generally because people start to notice the positive benefits that volunteering returns to them.

Obviously, the point of volunteering is to contribute your effort and intention to others or the environment. However, volunteering is not an entirely selfless act, regardless of how you justify it, and that is okay.

The benefits of volunteering can help you grow as an individual and increase your ability to continue to make a positive impact on the world. Volunteering can help you develop perspective-taking skills. As you work with people less fortunate than you, you begin to understand the world through a lens that you had not previously encountered. This expanded perspective will benefit you in school and in your relationships.

Volunteering can help you develop self-esteem and improve your self-worth. It feels good to help others. Volunteering can help improve your social skills and help you make new friends. And as we discussed earlier, volunteering can help you identify some crucial vocational skills that you may not be able to develop anywhere else. Volunteering also presents you in your greatest light to a network of potential future employers or advocates.

There are a variety of ways you can find volunteer opportunities. First and foremost, think of what kind of volunteering activities might interest you. This will hopefully align with your career interests, but it doesn't have to. It's more important that you find a volunteer opportunity that will motivate you to attend, as you can get the benefits from this experience even if it is outside of your career interests. If you want to be a lawyer but love animals, working for the Humane Society will still be a great opportunity. Once you've got some inspirations in mind, you can do a search for non-profits that support that area of interest. Once you've identified and researched programs that interest you, contact them directly to learn their volunteer roles. Most colleges also have a volunteer fair or a volunteer center that can provide information about different opportunities and even help you arrange the experience. You should aim to volunteer roughly 8-12 hours a month.

In most cities, there are lots of volunteer placements. Generally, most non-profit organizations are looking for volunteers, but also many government and healthcare organizations provide volunteer opportunities.

Here is a list of organizations that rely on volunteers and will happily put you to work:

Organization	Type of Work
YMCA	Childcare, customer service, custodial
Humane Society	Work with and care for animals
Habitat for Humanity	Build and remodel homes
Local food pantry	Collect and sort food and other supplies
Ronald McDonald House	Support families with children in the hospital

Local hospital	Various tasks supporting the hospital
Boys and Girls Club	Work with children
Local churches	Various tasks
Red Cross	Customer service
Local Museums	Various tasks
Retirement home	Various tasks while spending time with people like your grandparents
Goodwill or Salvation Army	Sorting and organizing donations
Political Campaigns	Supporting the candidate of your choice
Local parks and pools	Maintenance, customer service
Capitol or city hall	Various tasks
Your college	Various tasks right outside your door

Punching the Clock

Finding part-time paid employment in college is a decision that every student needs to consider carefully. For many students who are paying for college with loans or all on their own, getting a part time job may be necessary to afford a reasonable lifestyle. However, keep in mind, that when you decided to go to college, you also agreed to enter into voluntary poverty. Therefore, if you need to get a part time job, consider working only as much as you might need to get by. Your college experience is an investment in your future earnings, so school should be your focus now, not work. If your job is getting in the way of your studies you may have to consider alternative arrangements, such as working full time in the summer or taking out loans. However, if you find a good balance of your part time job and your studies, this a great opportunity for you to continue to develop your vocational skills, while also earning a little cash.

Future employers love to see that you have consistent, reference-worthy work experience, even if it involved delivering pizza.

Work study is another great opportunity to develop vocational skills, while also earning some cash. Work study is a federal program for students who are in financial need to earn money through jobs around campus. These jobs can be mundane jobs in the cafeteria or other campus facilities, or possibly jobs that are more specific to your career, such as research labs or field study. These jobs help to directly offset the cost of college and considering they are offered by the college; they may be more forgiving over the need for flexibility for your college schedule. Most campuses have an office dedicated to work study opportunities, so this may be a great place to start.

Your Foot in the Door

Finally, and most importantly is the need to find at least one college internship opportunity. College internships are the final experience in many majors and they are meant to prepare students for the transition to a career in their major. In fact, many major companies across the country are actually using the internship experience as an extended job interview, and hire students based on their performance as an intern. One of the greatest benefits of a college internship is that you will likely be able to earn college credit for it, and some internships will even pay you too.

Internships may be one of the most important experiences in college and therefore are often the most competitive in many fields. You'll want to contact the internship office on campus early in your college career to learn about the internship opportunities. Although you probably won't be eligible for many internships until later in college, you should see what opportunities may be available sooner.

Proving Your Work Ethic

With any of these vocational opportunities, you need to remember that whether you are working for free, getting paid, or earning credit, the most important thing that you are building is a track record. Each employer that you hope to work with will likely contact employers you list on your resume. Thus, each job you have will help you to get a better job in the future. If you don't take a job seriously, even a volunteer position, you will be at a disadvantage for the next job you hope to acquire. If you get fired from a job, or even worse a volunteer placement, you will lose that reference and your negative reputation may precede you. Take every vocational opportunity very seriously and give it your all.

Things to consider:

- When applying for a job, follow the directions carefully on how to apply. Be sure that anything you provide in your application is free of spelling and grammatical errors. Have someone double check your application. Employers who get applications with spelling or grammatical errors usually file them in the circular bin, i.e., the trash can, fairly quickly.

- If you get invited to an interview, it is important you show up to your interview on time and dressed professionally. It doesn't matter if you are applying to a fast-food restaurant or the White House, you should dress in business attire. Obviously, you don't need a three-piece suit for most college job interviews, but you should do your best to look nice.

- Always always always send a note to thank the person who interviewed you within 24 hours of the appointment. This could be an email or a card you drop by the office. Regardless, interviewers always look for that thank you note and it makes a big difference. Thank them for taking the time to interview you, remind the interviewers of one exciting dialogue from the interview and express your enthusiasm for the potential of working with them.

- If you receive the job, be sure to schedule a meeting with your future supervisor or send an email and ask about workplace expectations. You should be aware of the dress code, the schedule, and other important information about the position before you arrive on your first day.

- Don't be late. Being late to work is one of the biggest frustrations for any supervisor and it is always asked about in future reference checks. Show up early if you have to. If you know for sure that you will be late, call before you are late and let your supervisor know. When you arrive at work, apologize to your supervisor and let them know the steps you will take to avoid being late in the future.
- Ask for feedback regularly. Often times, the only way you'll know if you are doing a good is to ask. Schedule a check in with your supervisor and simply ask if there is anything you can improve on. If there are aspects of your job that you are confused about or are struggling with, address this with your supervisor immediately.
- If you realize at some point during your job that it's not a good fit and you believe it would be best to find a new position, always give two-week's notice. Sit down with your supervisor and explain that you've decided to seek different employment and are giving them two-week notice to replace you. Even if they are upset that you are leaving, they will respect you for giving them two weeks' notice. Never just walk off your job or stop showing up. It is one of the worst things you can do, as it greatly burdens the employer and usually makes them quite angry. (FYI: the "2 weeks' notice" courtesy is not always reciprocated; some businesses will terminate your job with your notification, so in making this decision, don't presume you will have 2 more weeks of pay.)
- Always ask for a letter of recommendation before leaving a job. You should also ask if future employers could contact them for a reference. It's much harder to get a letter of recommendation once you've left the position and if your direct supervisor moves along before you get the letter, you may never receive one. If your now-former boss doesn't have time to write one for you, she/he may be willing to sign something you "ghostwrite" (you write, honestly, about your positive employment experience, and then your supervisor signs it, as if they wrote it). Most employers like

to have three letters of recommendation when you apply, so start saving them.

Take-Aways:

- Build your vocational skills through real world opportunities.
- Volunteering is a must to be successful in college.
- Internships are often extended interviews, so seek them out.

CHAPTER 17:

Paying for it All

"Leaving college with a quarter million in debt and a degree in philosophy may not be the smartest way to begin adulthood."

R *ecently, I ran into a friend of mine from high school at a bar. We were pretty good friends in high school and connected over our shared desire to go into nursing. He was much better at school than I was, so when it came time to choose colleges, he had a few more options. At the time, I remember feeling extremely jealous of him as he prepared his applications for fancy East Coast colleges with prestigious names. I applied to every college in the state that had a nursing program. On Senior night, he garnered significant applause when they announced his name and his fancy school. Me, not so much.*

We began catching up about the past six years and where life has led us. I was surprised to hear that we were working for the same hospital system, just on opposite sides of town. I told him about the small house I purchased, the trips I've been taking, and the new car I had just purchased. I wasn't bragging, well, I suppose I was trying to prove to him that despite my high school performance, I was able to pull it together. When I asked him what he has been up to, I got a very different story.

He went on to tell me that he was living at home and taking the bus to work to save money. I was a bit shocked at first, seeing that we were probably being paid the same amount and I had plenty of money to play with. Then the reason came out: he was buried under debt. Apparently, he had paid for his fancy college with student loans and racked up a whopping $200,000 in debt. He had just started to pay the loans back and was paying about $1200 a month. I was dumbfounded.

I ended up earning my nursing degree at one of the smaller state schools a few hours from my house, where I was offered some tuition assistance. The education was excellent and very hands on, and honestly, probably a little less demanding than his expensive college. Plus, between some help from my family and some part-time employment, I was able to pay for my college as I went. I ended up with zero debt and the same job as my old, smart friend. I suppose the only difference between us now is that if we actually had offices, he could hang his fancy diploma up…if he could afford the frame.

Jody, *24, Nurse*

It is not uncommon to hear the phrase "college isn't for everyone". Given the huge costs of college and the associated debts, it's certainly something to carefully consider. Obviously, one big aspect of reading this book is determining whether college is right for you. It can't write you a golden ticket to paradise. Going to college for the sake of going to college is not a wise, or long-term, decision. In most countries, students take some time off to be kids and run around the world until they are ready to commit to college, they call it gap year (even the Amish built in an "excused absence" for adolescents called Rumspringa, a time to contemplate a mature dedication to the Amish existence).

However, if you know why you want to attend college or to simply continue to learn, then college is absolutely your right to pursue. However, with anything in life, there will be a cost-benefit analysis you should perform to determine how much college will cost, compared to your future. Leaving college with a quarter million in debt and a degree in philosophy may not be the smartest way to begin adulthood. So, it's extremely important that you think about how you are going to pay for college and be realistic about whether that specific degree will be worth the money.

First off, as we discussed earlier, there are a ton of great options for college. Moreover, the prices fluctuate greatly between those options. Some private schools can cost over $60,000 a year in tuition alone — this doesn't include a clothing budget, room or board while many community colleges are extremely affordable or totally free. So, you need to consider your access to financial support and whether paying more money is worth it.

In some careers, getting a degree from a prestigious or at least well-regarded university is necessary to compete in your field. For example, if you want to go to medical school, you'll probably need to complete your pre-med requirements in a "good" school, whereas there are other fields that are in such need, they'll hire qualified people from any school. There is currently a huge nursing shortage, for example, so a degree from an Ivy League college vs. your local state school will probably both end up in the same job, with the same salary, while it will take decades to pay off your Ivy League debt. And for what, a piece of paper to hang on your wall?

However, the debt you accrue at a more expensive school that increases your likelihood of getting into a medical school may be an excellent investment if you end up being a cardiologist. Determining the value of any particular college is completely up to you, but be realistic, this is an investment that should not financially cripple the successful graduate.

There are a variety of different ways to pay for college. You should consider all of them and be wise in developing a strategy to fund your degree. Most students rely on a variety of funding sources and strategies to pay for college. Your goal will be to finish college with as little debt as possible. Perhaps even, with no debt at all. This may not be easy or even possible, so limiting the amount of money that needs to be paid back with interest will set you up for the smoothest transition into your career. Consider all of your options and what combinations of resources might make the most sense for you.

Your Parents' Savings

For those of you who are fortunate enough to have a family who has saved money for your college degree, then you have much less to worry about. However, this doesn't mean you should blow your family's fortune on college. Discuss with your parents how much they are willing to spend on college each year. This may help you narrow down what colleges you can afford and if you will need to find additional money to offset the costs of more expensive colleges. If your parents are willing to pay a larger amount for college than you think you might need, you can always negotiate for more spending money or money toward savings if you go to a college that costs less.

For those of you whose family has not saved for your college degree, it still may be worth a conversation about what you as a family could do to pay for college that would be better than taking out student loans. Could your parents cover the cost of college and you agree to pay them back later? Do they own property that they could leverage to take out low interest loans that you pay back after college? Will your grandparents help pay for college? Is there a trust that you could access now to pay for college, instead of getting that money later? These are all great questions to explore with your family. If your family can pay for college without going to a lender, you could save a lot of money over time. (A financial planner may be helpful in considering all of your options.)

Obviously, not every student will be able to rely on parents who can pay for four years out of pocket. However, college is almost always a family endeavor. Having a frank conversation about how things will be paid for is important. The earlier you start with that conversation, the better.

Scholarships Support What You Do

There is a ton of free money out there that can help offset the cost of college. Your high school should have a list of scholarships that you can apply for locally. You should apply for as many applicable scholarships as you can find. Additionally, you should consider unique aspects of your life that may have scholarship money associated with it. Are there scholarships for your disability or diverse learning needs? For example, Autism Speaks has tons of money for students on the spectrum. Does your family identify as an ethnic minority? Did either of your parents serve in the military? Do you identify as lesbian, bisexual, gay, or transgendered? Do your parents work for a large corporation? Will you pursue college athletics? All of these situations may make you eligible for a college scholarship. Additionally, there is a huge list of college scholarships available at www.collegescholarships.org. Remember, if you meet and maintain the scholarship's structure, it is free cash toward tuition.

Grants Support Who You Are

The difference between grants and scholarships is that although neither need to be paid back, scholarships are usually merit or performance-based, whereas grants are need-based. If you qualify for financial assistance, there is a lot of grant money to help support your college endeavors. You should start by filling out a Free Application for Federal Student Aid or more commonly referred to as FAFSA. This will evaluate your eligibility for financial assistance in federal, state, and private programs. You can find everything you need at www.fafsa.ed.gov. Additionally, there are a variety of services available to help you navigate through the various scholarships and grants. For example, NextGen Vest is a service that helps potential college students plan to pay for college. There is also a plethora of great websites that help you find the money you need.

Ask for It

Many colleges today are facing low enrollment and increased pressure on admissions. The worst marketing for a college is to hear that they are short students or that their numbers have been decreasing. Thus, lots of colleges are greatly reducing the cost of tuition for specific students through scholarships or grants from the college, just to get you in the dorm room door. When you begin your college application process, be sure to ask every college if they have scholarships or grants to offset the tuition. If they accept your application, they may offer you some financial assistance, but whether they do or don't, you should always ask for more financial help. Often, if they know you will accept if they offer you more money, they will do what they can. You can also play schools against one another, by letting them know how much another college has offered you in scholarships. The majority of college students are receiving some free money from the college they are attending.

Student Loans Are a Short-Term Solution

The final, probably worst, but certainly most necessary option for some people is taking out student loans. Roughly 71% of students who graduate from a four-year university have student loan debt[14]. Additionally, student loan debt in this country is over one trillion dollars. The average debt of a student graduating from a private college is almost $40,000. What's even worse is that over 60% of students didn't understand the terms of their loan when they took it out and found out too late that they had signed up for loans with unfavorable interest rates and payment schedules.

Obviously, if you can avoid acquiring student loans, you should. However, student loans are just a necessity for many people who want to attend college so you should be vigilant about them. There are a variety of places you can learn about the various student loan options, such as www.studentloans.gov, but you can also go to a local bank or credit union to learn about the various student loan options.

---

14   www.millennialmoneyman.com

If you need to rely on student loans, there are some general rules you should consider. First, apply for as much free scholarship and grant money as possible through the programs we discussed above. These options don't require you to pay them back and don't compound interest every year. Apply for federal loans first before applying for private loans. The rates and terms are usually better. You can see which federal loans are available when you complete your FAFSA.

Alert! Don't take on more debt over your college career than you reasonably anticipate your salary will be in the first year of your intended profession.

If you plan on working for the government or a non-profit, depending on your loan terms, you may be eligible for Public Service Loan Forgiveness, so research this early in the process.

Finally, only take out what you will need. Most lenders will happily give you as much as you request, they know you think it's free money. But for the bank, it's a huge profit. Be realistic about what you can get by on. Be frugal and think of ways to borrow less. Most importantly, live within your means. Don't spend more than you have. College loans are not free money, they are actually a very expensive financial straitjacket immediately after graduation.

Take-Aways:

- Have a frank conversation with your family about how you'll pay for college.
- Apply for every scholarship and grant that is available to you.
- Use student loans sparingly and wisely.

CHAPTER 18:

You Can Do It

"Whatever your diverse learning needs, disabilities or potential strengths are, they pale in comparison to the inner drive that is waiting to be tapped that provides you the fortitude to overcome any obstacle that lies in front of you."

At the beginning of this book, you met Drew Maxwell. Drew's story wasn't the Hollywood-stereotypical college success story of a student with a disability, nor was it intended to be. If what inspires you are stories about Bill Gates having autism or Albert Einstein having a learning disability, then by all means indulge yourself. But for most of us, we are no Albert Einstein or Bill Gates, nor will we ever be. We are just regular people with some unique strengths and ordinary challenges doing our best to enjoy life. College isn't going to be a Cinderella story for you, like it wasn't a Cinderella story for Drew. No one will carry you across the stage on their shoulders when and if you graduate. No one will think you beat all the odds to get your diploma. And certainly, college won't be a walk in the park for *you*, seeing as it's not a walk in the park for *anyone*. What's remarkable about Drew's story isn't in his success, but in his struggle. It's not in his traditional path to his career, but his exceptional path that makes his story interesting. It's not his disability that makes him remarkable, it's in his refusal to take no for an answer, his creative development of options to significant obstacles and in his unwavering determination to get what he wanted out of life. Drew's story is remarkable because it's actually the everyday story of someone who did what it took to succeed, regardless of the odds. Drew's simple mantra that fueled each step was simply, "I can do it."

You can do it. That's the only thing you need to believe when starting on your journey to college. 'You can do it' doesn't imply that you'll do it the way you expected to, in the timeframe you were hoping for, in the way others do it, or without also putting in all extra work and focus and strategies this book has recommended. 'You can do it' implies that there are only divergences of trails ahead of you and no dead ends. 'You can do it' implies that when someone says no, you find the *yes* in their response, and if they close the door, you open the window. 'You can do it' implies that getting what you want never involves giving up on what you want, only finding the path that is right for you. 'You can do it' implies that you believe in yourself more than you believe in anyone or anything in the world. You can do it, because you believe you can do it. You can do it.

Taking flight is no simple task, whether you are a fledgling, one of the Wright Brothers, or taking flight into adulthood. It's filled with missteps, stumbles, battered bones and bruised egos. Giving up results in the rest of the world flying by you, when you were meant to be flying with the world. But giving up is not an option. We were born to fly and deep within our DNA is a drive that is relentless to launch us on a path of joy and success. Whatever your diverse learning needs, disabilities or potential strengths are, they pale in comparison to the inner drive that is waiting to be tapped that provides you the fortitude to overcome any obstacle that lies in front of you. You must believe that you will fly, you must believe that you were destined to fly, and you need to commit yourself to the pursuit of your flight. You will likely enjoy the view more than others, fly in ways that inspire those who come after you, and share the meaningful flight you create with those around you.

If there is only one thing you that you take away from reading this book, hopefully it is really believing that the horizon in front of you is only limited by the limits you place on yourself, that any other limit is someone else's false belief. You are reading this book because you have overcome the odds, you have out-maneuvered expectations, and you are sitting at the edge of a decision to finally prove to yourself, and no one else, that you deserve the dignity of your self-determination. You deserve the right to blaze your own path and relentlessly pursue your dreams. You deserve the right to fail at times, as much as you deserve the right to brush yourself off and learn from each misstep. You deserve the right to unapologetically be you and not the deficits assigned to you by others. You deserve this opportunity. You can do it.

Take-Away:

- You can do it.

ACKNOWLEDGMENTS

Writing a book and sharing the insights I've gained from my life and work with Mansfield Hall was never something I would have considered without the encouragement (coercion) from my dear friend and colleague Jake Weld. More importantly, I'd like to thank him for his willingness to hear my ideas, read early versions, and provide his valuable revisions, perspectives, and edits.

I'd like to thank the people who took the time to read several early drafts of this book and provide me with their valuable feedback — Nick Adler, Alix Generous, Jill and Jordan Burstein of JJB Consulting, and Marybeth Kravets of Marybeth Kravets & Associates.

Thank you to my editors Patrick Logan and Todd Porter for their help editing, revising, formatting, and providing their valuable input.

I'd like to thank Michael Ebeling for connecting me to the excellent team at Morgan James Publishing. Specifically, I'd like to thank David Hancock, CEO of Morgan James, and Gayle West for their confidence and enthusiasm for this project.

My sincerest appreciation to all of the staff, students, and families of Mansfield Hall, especially Jasmine Lamb and Sara Adsit. You are living and breathing the challenges and joys of higher education every day and are not only changing lives, but transforming the institutions and paving the way for future deserving students.

I'd like to thank my family — my Mom for always believing in me, my Dad for always pushing me, my sister for always having my back, and everyone else for bringing humor, love, and passion to my life.

I would not be where I am today without the love, support, and confidence of my gracious in-laws, Connie Ganapes and Jim Mazzulla. Thank you.

Thank you to my (big) brother, Sean LaRoque, for being my best friend, business partner, and voice of reason. Mansfield Hall would not be what it is today without your partnership.

Finally, I'd like to thank my amazing wife, Emily Mazzulla, for always seeing my potential and not letting me settle for less. And, my wonderful and spirited children, James, Georgia, and Teddy, who are always providing me with the best excuse to procrastinate.

ABOUT THE AUTHOR

Perry LaRoque is the Founder and President of Mansfield Hall, an innovative residential college support program for students with autism spectrum disorders and other related learning differences, located in Burlington, VT, Madison, WI and Eugene, OR. Prior to launching Mansfield Hall, Perry co-founded the College Steps Program and was involved in developing the Think College programs in Vermont. He also served as a special education professor at Johnson State College, SUNY-Potsdam, and UW-Whitewater. Before completing his doctorate in Special Education at the University of Wisconsin, Perry was a special education teacher in California and Wisconsin. He currently resides in Milwaukee, WI with his wife and three children.

Please visit www.perrylaroque.com for additional resources, upcoming speaking engagements, and to contact him directly.

A free ebook edition is available with the purchase of this book.

To claim your free ebook edition:

1. Visit MorganJamesBOGO.com
2. Sign your name CLEARLY in the space
3. Complete the form and submit a photo of the entire copyright page
4. You or your friend can download the ebook to your preferred device

Morgan James BOGO™

A **FREE** ebook edition is available for you
or a friend with the purchase of this print book.

CLEARLY SIGN YOUR NAME ABOVE

Instructions to claim your free ebook edition:
1. Visit MorganJamesBOGO.com
2. Sign your name CLEARLY in the space above
3. Complete the form and submit a photo
   of this entire page
4. You or your friend can download the ebook
   to your preferred device

Print & Digital Together Forever.

Snap a photo

Free ebook

Read anywhere